GUIDED MEDITATION

Learn Energy Healing Techniques With Guided Meditations

(A Powerful Guidebook to Improve Now Your Mindfulness and Self-healing)

Maggie Hernandez

Published by Alex Howard

Maggie Hernandez

All Rights Reserved

Guided Meditation: Learn Energy Healing Techniques With Guided Meditations (A Powerful Guidebook to Improve Now Your Mindfulness and Self-healing)

ISBN 978-1-77485-072-5

All rights reserved. No part of this guide may be reproduced in any form without permission in writing from the publisher except in the case of brief quotations embodied in critical articles or reviews.

Legal & Disclaimer

The information contained in this book is not designed to replace or take the place of any form of medicine or professional medical advice. The information in this book has been provided for educational and entertainment purposes only.

The information contained in this book has been compiled from sources deemed reliable, and it is accurate to the best of the Author's knowledge; however, the Author cannot guarantee its accuracy and validity and cannot be held liable for any errors or omissions. Changes are periodically made to this book. You must consult your doctor or get professional medical advice before using any of the suggested remedies, techniques, or information in this book.

Upon using the information contained in this book, you agree to hold harmless the Author from and against any damages, costs, and expenses, including any legal fees potentially resulting from the application of any of the information provided by this guide. This disclaimer applies to any damages or injury caused by the use and application, whether directly or indirectly, of any advice or information presented, whether for breach of contract, tort, negligence, personal injury, criminal intent, or under any other cause of action.

You agree to accept all risks of using the information presented inside this book. You need to consult a professional medical practitioner in order to ensure you are both able and healthy enough to participate in this program.

Table of Contents

INTRODUCTION 1

CHAPTER 1: WHAT CONDITIONS US? 9

CHAPTER 2: LAW OF CAUSE AND EFFECT 16

CHAPTER 3: THE LIGHT WARRIOR MEDITATION 25

CHAPTER 4: GUIDED MEDITATIONS FOR LETTING GO FEAR 41

CHAPTER 5: THIRD WEEK OF MEDITATIONS 59

CHAPTER 6: THE IMPORTANCE OF MEDITATION 105

CHAPTER 7: SLEEP SCRIPTS 111

CHAPTER 8: COUNTERING ANXIETY THROUGH MEDITATION TECHNIQUES 124

CHAPTER 9: HOW TO START MEDITATING 142

CHAPTER 10: 50 DAILY AFFIRMATIONS TO PROMOTE POSITIVE THINKING 156

CHAPTER 11: IMPROVE YOUR RELATIONSHIP WITH WORK | 10 MINUTES | 1000 WORDS 180

CONCLUSION 193

Introduction

Do you frequently find yourself unable to fall asleep even when you are extremely fatigued? Are you able to fall asleep but keep getting up in the middle of the night? Or maybe you get satisfactory quality of sleep on some days, but the rest of the week is bad? Or maybe you can only get 4-5 hours of sleep every night. If you answered yes to one or more of the above, you might have a chronic sleep problem like insomnia and others Yeah, if you're having difficulty getting asleep at night, you're surely not isolated here. Hundreds of people across the world experience sleep issues. About 35 to 50 percent of every adult around the world experience symptoms of insomnia on a regular basis.

In the rapidly growing, fast-paced world of the 21st century, insomnia, and the resultant sleep deprivation have reached the level of a pandemic. It is much more prevalent than we think. Its consequences are far-reaching and affect our waking life too.

Nowadays, it seems impossible to get some adequate shut-eye every night. It is actually getting harder and harder to relax and wind down at the end of each day, since we all face the evils of rumination, worrying excessively. And, the implications of insomnia and other sleep disorders are pretty clear for all those who suffer from it. Since a good, rejuvenating night sleep is always a precursor to a better, fresher day, the consistent absence or lack of an adequate night sleep becomes a bigger problem. Sleep deprivation has been found to be associated with depression, heart disease, schizophrenia, chronic fatigue syndrome, cancer, stroke, Parkinson's disease, and even Alzheimer's disease.

Hence, it transcends the confines of being a sleeping problem to also becoming a day time problem as well. The way you act when awake depends in part on what happens when you sleep. The body works during sleep to promote healthy brain activity and preserve physical health. Sleep also helps to promote the growth and development of children and adolescents. Considering the ravages of insomnia, it becomes imperative for one to try to fix this problem. This is where guided meditation can prove to be an absolute gem.

There can be many causes of insomnia, which we will discuss in detail in chapter 2. But, for most of the world's population, the sleeping difficulty is linked to stress, anxiety, and rumination. And, stress can cause tension and anxiety, keeping it way harder to sleep for people as compared to someone who is not as stressed. In most cases, stress can normally worsen previous sleep issues.

It is projected that about 50 and 70 million Americans regularly suffer from a condition of wakefulness and sleep, impeding normal life and adversely impacting wellbeing and lifespan.

There are about 90 distinct sleep disorders; most of them are characterized by one of the following symptoms: prolonged daytime sleepiness, difficulty in initiating or managing sleep, and irregular sleep occurrences. A number of negative health outcomes, like increased risk of diabetes, hypertension, obesity, stroke, heart attack, and depression, have been correlated with sleep deprivation and sleep disorders. After decades of study, the case can be made sure that there are significant and widespread effects of sleep deprivation and sleep disorders on human health. A number of negative health and social effects, including poor results at school and in the workplace, are also correlated with inadequate sleep.

Sleep plays a crucial role in your entire life in good health and well-. Having good quality sleep at the right time will help protect your mental health, physical health, quality of life, and safety. The damage caused by the sleep deficit can occur in an instant (such as a car crash), or over time it can affect you. Perpetual sleep deprivation, for example, may increase the risk of certain chronic health problems.

This can also influence how well you think, how well you respond, how you function, how you learn, and how you get along with others.

If insomnia is at the root of your sleepless nights, guided meditation is an excellent resource. It has been shown that the deep relaxation technique increases sleep time, enhances sleep quality, and makes it easier to fall as well as stay asleep. These are some key facts about the procedure that may help you resolve any reluctance about trying it.

Driven meditation will help you sleep well and ward off those nights of sleeplessness. It will calm the body and mind while fostering inner harmony as a calming strategy. Mindfulness may help to minimize anxiety and sleep disruptions by encouraging complete calmness when performed before bedtime.

Guided sleep meditation is a way to help you let go of stressful thoughts and calm your body before bed. As with other types of meditation, this practice includes turning the attention away from your mind to your body's sensations. It has been shown that daily practice of guided sleep meditation enhances sleep, suggesting that this technique is an effective tool that you can use to help minimize problems regarding falling and staying asleep.

Better sleep can help to lower stress and strengthen the immune system. However, if you're battling tension and anxiety, finding restful sleep can be hard— it can be just hard to quiet your mind. Many problems surrounding sleep start at night with your thought processes. There's where guided meditation on sleep will improve.

Guided sleep meditation is pretty safe. It is a great tool for people who are trying an all-natural, medication-free way of treating insomnia. In reality, the use of sleeping pills has also been shown to help minimize meditation. The practice undoubtedly improves symptoms of insomnia by reducing brain arousal mechanisms. And there are no complications or side effects related to attempting meditation. It can be used with other techniques as well. It has been shown that a mix of cognitive-behavioral therapy used for insomnia (CBT-I) and mindfulness meditation enhances sleep better than CBT-I alone. The health benefits are numerous. Meditation can not only enhance the quality of your sleep, but it can also help to lower blood pressure and relieve discomfort, anxiety, and depression.

Guided sleep meditation is an affordable, budget-friendly practice that anyone can do. Insomnia sufferers of all ages, including older adults, respond well to the practice. You can pay for the meditative classes and books that teach you the techniques. Or you can also search online for free apps and YouTube videos for guided sleep meditations.

This book is a step-by-step guide on how to use guided meditation before bed for better sleep and fight insomnia. The chapters will entail the basics of guided meditation, how it is different from unguided meditation and hypnosis. It will also include a dedicated chapter on insomnia, its causes, and other sleep disorders. Then, we'll discuss the benefits of anxiety, overthinking, and stress, along with some relaxation techniques for sleep. Finally, the last chapter will include details on guided sleep meditations using hypnosis, binaural beats, and other techniques.

Chapter 1: What Conditions Us?

Personal Perspective and Opinion
We are all aware of certain aspects of our own perspective. For example, you know very well whether or not you think pizza and ice cream are tasty. Some people believe that these are disgusting because they don't like drinking milk or eating cheese. Others believe that they could survive on these two foods alone. You might think those action movies are the best genre. Then there are others who would rather watch romantic comedies all day.
Some individuals enjoy playing music. Others would prefer to spend their time reading and writing.
These all seem as though they create our perspectives, but they are really more based on our opinions. Opinions are essential to have. While it is good to be objective in certain circumstances, we also have to consider the fact that our opinion

is really based on who we are as individuals. Opinion creates a unique character that helps us to find our individuality. The world would be a really dull place if we all agreed on the same things all the time. While some opinions might actually damage people in the long run, such as the opinion that certain types of people can't get married or others don't deserve as many rights, there are still plenty of positive aspects to opinions that create the beautiful and diverse world in which we thrive.

At the same time, as these opinions are making up what our perspective is, we also have to understand our viewpoint deeply because it's like the set of glasses that we look through. If you looked through a pair of red glasses all the time, everything would seem to be a particular color. If you looked through blue lenses, it would be a different shade. Our perspective isn't always as distinct as a pair of blue or red glasses; a number of many things create your perspective. We have to understand how our view interferes with our ability to communicate and interpret communication from other people.

First and foremost, we have to understand that what we were taught will define our perspective. There are tons of people who are trained to keep their mouth shut and not to say anything whatsoever. Then there are others who are taught that they're allowed to say whatever they want all the time, regardless of who they might be hurting in the process. Then there are the individuals who are taught healthy communication and are given a chance sometimes to express themselves and also be given proper tools to make communication a little bit easier.

When it comes to our perspective, we also have to remember that we will have individual goals and desires for ourselves, and because of those specific aspects of life will seem more important or less important. For example, if your purpose in life is to be a celebrity, and have millions of dollars, then your perspective is different from somebody who's goal is only to do scientific research and study the greater truth in life.

The individual who was obsessed with the idea of money will often look at material things, more so than symbolic elements. A psychologist who's always conducting research is going to be looking for the more profound meaning and greater truth of everything that they come in contact with. The greedy person is then going to have a skewed perspective when they meet a new individual, rather than discussing and talking to them about certain things, they'll look at what they're wearing or how they might have done their hair. They'll use this as a way to judge them.

How we judge and perceive other people are always going to be different from others.

When you are looking for a new person, you'll pull them from the information that will give you greater insight into who they really are. Our brains work in such a way that they're continually taking new information and applying it to things that we already know. This is most easily done through symbolic elements. Our perception will also be based on our emotional state. Some individuals are a little bit more sensitive and might be more likely to get angry with those around them. Other individuals might have a very fresh perspective, and they have patience and understanding that makes it easy for them to withhold judgment. The emotional state that you're feeling, not just today, but in the exact moment that you're talking to somebody can make you understand the other person differently. For example, let's say that you had a horrible day. Everything is annoying you, and nothing seems to be going right when you're talking to somebody. As you pick up on what they're saying and study their body language, you are going to be looking for signs within this communicative state that validate that negative perspective that you've had all day.

Rather than sitting there and listening to the words they say objectively, you're already pretty annoyed, so if they do something slightly irritating, it's going to seem even worse to you.

At the same time, we also frequently look for signs that validate the things that we already believe.

For example, let's say that you have a crush on somebody. Maybe it's the cute boy working at the local coffee shop. You go in every day to order a new coffee. Some days you feel really anxious about yourself; you have low self-esteem, and you think that you are unattractive and undesirable and on those days you go into the coffee shop when you have the interaction with this cute boy you're going to pick up on things that validate your low self-esteem. You're going to notice that he might not look at you. Maybe he seems dismissive perhaps there's another girl in there that he gives more attention to. Then there are days where you feel incredibly confident. Maybe you got a new hairstyle and a new outfit, and you generally feel excellent about yourself. You think that you're beautiful and there's nothing that's going to kill this mood. Then when you go and order your coffee, the guy behind the counter seems a little bit more flirtatious; maybe you pick up that he made eye contact with you or that he commented on your new hair. You are going to take in everything he does that validates the perspective that you are beautiful. What we don't realize is that this person is probably acting the same every day. We're just looking at different parts of their behavior to validate our perspective. In reality, this coffee boy does like you and thinks you're cute, but he also has his perspectives, wherein he picks up on different things from you. We have to be very aware of our view and how it can cause us to misinterpret information in order to get a better understanding of what the objective truth is. When you are trying to analyze somebody else's body language, always consider if there is an underlying thought or emotion that might be influencing the reading that you're taking from them.

Chapter 2: Law Of Cause And Effect

One important part of meditation that people don't actually discuss as well the law of cause and effect or even called karma. You might know what this is because you've heard of something, and you may have been told that "oh that's karma"! And wonder just what in the world that even means. Well, you're about to find out. Here, we'll talk about this, and just how it applies to the different relaxation skills.

What is it?

Essentially, karma is the idea that every single action generates an equal or opposite force that's similar in some way. Essentially, we reap what we sow, and we choose the actions that bring happiness, and success, and that in turn will allow karma to help breed the same happiness and success.

Why does this matter in relaxation? Well, lots of times, if we fall into the trap of thinking that we don't need to take the time to get comfortable and have a guided message of comfort or discomfort, you're going to end up continually being uncomfortable. Lots of times, we don't even realize that small things we do can change the way karma, or the law of cause and effect, swings within or against our favor. In the small witness of choice, you can choose whether you want to bring conscious awareness or not. You'll want to, with karma, understand how to be fully conscious that your actions have an equal reaction to what might happen in the future.

If you cause good things, you'll bring forth good things.

How this plays into life

Lots of times, we bog ourselves down with the idea that we can't relax, that stress and anxiety are going to be the lot of us, and we're never going to be happy. I understand that life is hard. But, if you continually think that you can never get better, will you get better?

The answer is no.

People don't realize that a little bit of positive thinking, or choosing to plunge away from the negativity, can make a difference. Even the choice of leaving someone behind because they're not good for you is a prime example of putting the law of karma into effect.

Whatever you choose to do in life is going to produce a reaction, whether you like it or not, and whether it's something that you want or not. Everything in our world, on earth period, has a starting point. Every single path has an original first step that comes from this, and within it, a chain reaction of different events that come from offshoots spinning in different directions, and the duplication and replication of this does continue to happen as well.

Every single thought, every single element of human behavior, every single movement that you employ follows the laws of cause and effect. Everything is relative, and nothing is separate. Therefore, if you move your hand, you're moving it in a space, and that the space is connected within the universe.

Therefore, from this, we can conclude that every single inanimate object in this universe is connected within the space, and it occupies the same space in our mind. There isn't any separation of this, and if you're moving your hand, you're moving the space that's connected to this.

it's a weird concept, that's for sure, and you have to realize that it might take a minute to grasp this concept, but here's a general idea: everything that you do in this universe has always existed, and what you do in life will cause some sort of effect from this.

Human thought creates a movement, no matter how small it might be. You're essentially creating a movement no matter what you do. Every single movement that you have will relate to further thoughts over time. Every single movement that happens in our lives has some thought preceding it, and every movement is the result of a thought.

We mostly are all governed by this idea, and we are subject to the law of cause and effect, and we are the effect of the cause of the universe. Essentially, once you set an idea into the universe, it will create an effect in this, and you'll continue that ripple no matter what.

Nothing happens by chance. You might think it's the universe just screwing with you, or maybe it's fate just happening in a happenstance manner, but the truth is, at the end of every single action as well, a thought. No matter how specific, or how negative the situation might be, there is always a thought that comes from it. Every single thought that we throw into the universe will cause something to happen, whether it be good or bad.

An Example

Here is an excellent example of the law of cause and effect, that you're the creator of your own destiny. Do you sometimes feel like you can't control your stress or your anxiety? This is a common problem lots of people have, and while they may try different medications and the like, if they can't fully decide that hey, they want to be in control of this, it will continue to do down the pathway.

Remember, every single thought is what causes an action. Things don't just happen willy-nilly. People don't just decide to do things on a whim, and then they go from there. They're all decided by a thought.

So, if you feel like you're not making enough money, for example, look at your thought process. Do you feel like you can't ever make enough money? That you're always going to be in the red, no matter what the odds might be? If that's the case, you're going to end up creating a lot of trouble for yourself, and over time, you're going to end up creating more and more headaches for yourself too. For many people, realizing that they are in control of their destiny is something they might not be good at, but the law of cause and effect means that, if you want to create the results that you want, you need to cause it.

You can pray to a supernatural being for days on end, but the truth of it is, if you're not the one taking control of your destiny, you're never going to be happy. It's essential to realize that the one in control is you.

How this applies to anxiety

Now I'm not saying that you can just magically decide for your anxiety to go away, and then boom it does. That's not how it happens. But what you need to realize, is that you're the one in control of your own personal destiny, whether it is you are in control of yourself, or not. If you're sick of dealing with the stresses of life, then look at yourself, and figure out what is making you stress. If it's something in your life that is bothering you, then you should work to change this. If it's something that you can eliminate from your plate, or maybe just meditating to relax on, then start to do that. Remember, being in control of your own destiny will help you create good things.

Everything in life is caused by you, whether you like it or not. I know that life is full of ups and downs, but every single bad situation is caused by a previous thought that came beforehand. It can be anything from you're not sure if you'll make the team, or maybe you won't do well on this job. Whatever it might be, you're going to have a thought tailing the actions that happen.

So, what that means, is if you catch yourself thinking bad, or distracting thoughts, stop yourself. That's going to cause the actions to be wrong. It can be anything from realizing that hey, you're being distracted by negative thoughts, to even just stopping the negative thoughts in their tracks. Remember, if you're able to do this, to stop yourself from being negative, it will help you create a better life.

Karma, or cause and effect, is a big part of meditation too. If you take the time to change your life, you're going to end up creating a much healthier life. This is pretty true if you look at people who decide to make a change in their life, whether it be to be less stressed, to take care of their body, or whatnot. Being able to take care of yourself, and making the smart, righteous decisions that will help you, will allow you to create a better and healthier life that will allow you to decide for yourself what you can do in order to create a better life not just for yourself, but for others as well.

So yes, understand that your actions play a big part in the future that you create, and if you want to earn and reap the benefits of meditation honestly, understand that it doe start with yourself, the decision to get better, and the idea that you're going to create a healthier life from this as well.

Chapter 3: The Light Warrior Meditation

This third meditation combines the Body Scan meditation and the Meditation of the Sun, bringing you a deep sense of relax and relieving you from anxiety.

I have used this technique during the most difficult periods of my life and it has helped me to come up on top of things. That is why it has a special place in my heart and why I decided to share it in this book. I really want everyone to benefit from it.

First, we will start the meditation with a deep body scan, as shown in the very first technique of the book. We will take our time to go through it properly, as it will be our grounding phase and it plays an important role for the entire practice.

Secondly, we will spend some time performing the liquid sunlight exercise, as it will give us the ability to melt anxiety and stress away from our body.

Finally, we will direct our attention on loving and kind thoughts, which will be our priming for the rest of the day. Focusing on the good always attracts positive in our life, that is why the Light Warrior goes through life with good vibes and intentions: he knows the world is a mirror and will give him back what he brings to the world.

Let's get started!

Find a comfortable, relaxed and balanced position. Give yourself permission to be completely present for yourself, and let your body and mind calm down until they become soft and relaxed.

Breathe in, feel relaxed...
breathe out, feel calm...
Breathe in, feel relaxed...
breathe out, feel calm...
Breathe in, feel relaxed...
breathe out, feel calm...
Breathe in, feel relaxed...
breathe out, feel calm...

Allow the mind to distance itself from all thoughts and orientate awareness on your breath. Breathe naturally and do not force a specific rhythm. Let your breath come and go.

Carefully, now, drive your attention from the breath to the space in which you are.

Feel the energy and atmosphere of this space as it permeates all of your being. Notice the noises in the background. Maybe there is a clock ticking, maybe there are cars passing just outside your windows. Whatever you feel it is fine, let your attention rest on the external.

Breathe in, feel relaxed...
breathe out, feel calm...
Breathe in, feel relaxed...
breathe out, feel calm...
Breathe in, feel relaxed...
breathe out, feel calm...
Breathe in, feel relaxed...
breathe out, feel calm...

Now bring the attention back to the breath. Take your time and you will naturally reach a place of warmth and ease. Stay in this state where you feel your body and mind completely calm, relaxed and full of peace for a few minutes,

without letting go the focus on your breath.
Breathe in, feel relaxed...
breathe out, feel calm...
Breathe in, feel relaxed...
breathe out, feel calm...
Breathe in, feel relaxed...
breathe out, feel calm...
Breathe in, feel relaxed...
breathe out, feel calm...
Breathe in, feel relaxed...
breathe out, feel calm...
Breathe in, feel relaxed...
breathe out, feel calm...
Breathe in, feel relaxed...
breathe out, feel calm...
Breathe in, feel relaxed...
breathe out, feel calm...
Now, begin to scan your body from the bottom of your toes up to the top of your head. Do this slowly and stop on each part of your body to listen to what it has to tell you. If you feel contracted on a specific area, keep the attention on that part for as long as you feel it relaxing. It is important that you do not force this process, just

keep breathing and you will feel your body getting more and more relaxed.

Begin from your big toes, how do they feel today? Have you ever asked yourself this question? Pain a clear picture of them inside your head, as you slowly shift your attention to your ankles.

During this practice, each joint is a crucial point where anxiety can infiltrate itself. If you find a part of your body that feels tight, you can softly massage it with your hands until you feel it completely relaxed.

Breathe in, feel relaxed...
breathe out, feel calm...
Breathe in, feel relaxed...
breathe out, feel calm...
Breathe in, feel relaxed...
breathe out, feel calm...
Breathe in, feel relaxed...
breathe out, feel calm...

Reach your knees and feel them. How are your knees today? Maybe they are sore because you have been standing all day or made an effort yesterday. Maybe they are relaxed and strong. Whatever you feel, it is okay. Moving up your quadriceps, reach your pelvic floor and genital area.

This is an extremely crucial zone of your body when it comes to anxiety and stress, as a lot of energy is drawn down to it by your neuromuscular system. Spend a few minutes on your pelvic, before moving upwards. I will give you the time you need.

Breathe in, feel relaxed...
breathe out, feel calm...
Breathe in, feel relaxed...
breathe out, feel calm...
Breathe in, feel relaxed...
breathe out, feel calm...
Breathe in, feel relaxed...
breathe out, feel calm...
Breathe in, feel relaxed...
breathe out, feel calm...
Breathe in, feel relaxed...
breathe out, feel calm...
Breathe in, feel relaxed...
breathe out, feel calm...
Breathe in, feel relaxed...
breathe out, feel calm...
Breathe in, feel relaxed...
breathe out, feel calm...

Breathe in, feel relaxed...
breathe out, feel calm...
Breathe in, feel relaxed...
breathe out, feel calm...
Breathe in, feel relaxed...
breathe out, feel calm...
Keep going up, reaching your chest and your shoulders. This is where a lot of tension can be usually found, so take your time in this area. If you feel a bit stiff, do not hesitate to move your arms, until they reach a comfortable position. Feel your lungs and heart, still beating strong even if you had a rough day or are facing issues at the moment.
The heart keeps beating, the lungs keep breathing.
Breathe in, feel relaxed...
breathe out, feel calm...
Breathe in, feel relaxed...
breathe out, feel calm...
Breathe in, feel relaxed...
breathe out, feel calm...
Breathe in, feel relaxed...
breathe out, feel calm...
Breathe in, feel relaxed...

breathe out, feel calm...
Breathe in, feel relaxed...
breathe out, feel calm...
Breathe in, feel relaxed...
breathe out, feel calm...
Breathe in, feel relaxed...
breathe out, feel calm...

And finally you reach your head. Keep breathing into your head and feel the air slowly filling every empty space of your head.

How does the air feel? Is it cold or warm? What does it smell like? Do you like it? Those are all simple questions that we forget to ask ourself during the day, but that can help us ground ourself back into our body.

Breathe in, feel relaxed...
breathe out, feel calm...
Breathe in, feel relaxed...
breathe out, feel calm...
Breathe in, feel relaxed...
breathe out, feel calm...
Breathe in, feel relaxed...
breathe out, feel calm...

Stay in this beautiful space for as long as you want, you deserve it.
Breathe in, feel relaxed...
breathe out, feel calm...
Breathe in, feel relaxed...
breathe out, feel calm...
Breathe in, feel relaxed...
breathe out, feel calm...
Breathe in, feel relaxed...
breathe out, feel calm...
Breathe in, feel relaxed...
breathe out, feel calm...
Breathe in, feel relaxed...
breathe out, feel calm...
Breathe in, feel relaxed...
breathe out, feel calm...
Breathe in, feel relaxed...
breathe out, feel calm...
Breathe in, feel relaxed...
breathe out, feel calm...
Breathe in, feel relaxed...
breathe out, feel calm...
Breathe in, feel relaxed...
breathe out, feel calm...
Breathe in, feel relaxed...
breathe out, feel calm...

Breathe in, feel relaxed...
breathe out, feel calm...
Breathe in, feel relaxed...
breathe out, feel calm...
Breathe in, feel relaxed...
breathe out, feel calm...
Breathe in, feel relaxed...
breathe out, feel calm...
Now bring the attention back to the body and start feeling your arms and legs once again. You can close your hands or move your fingers, just to take control of the space around you.
Please, keep the eyes closed for now and enjoy the beautiful moment you are living. You have given yourself the time to feel better and that is absolutely incredible.
Breathe in, feel relaxed...
breathe out, feel calm...
Breathe in, feel relaxed...
breathe out, feel calm...
Breathe in, feel relaxed...
breathe out, feel calm...
Breathe in, feel relaxed...
breathe out, feel calm...

In your own time, try to imagine a sphere of liquid sunlight just a few inches above your head. Imagining a small sun can be beneficial during this part, as it helps your mind and body to adapt to this new entity. With every breath now, feel the liquid sunlight coming down into your head and through your spine, reaching the bottom of your feet through your pelvic floor and legs. Your body is getting filled with this warm and soft light. Can you feel it?

If you are struggling, it is fine, do not force it too much. It will get better over time.

Breathe in, feel relaxed...
breathe out, feel calm...
Breathe in, feel relaxed...
breathe out, feel calm...
Breathe in, feel relaxed...
breathe out, feel calm...
Breathe in, feel relaxed...
breathe out, feel calm...
Breathe in, feel relaxed...
breathe out, feel calm...
Breathe in, feel relaxed...
breathe out, feel calm...
Breathe in, feel relaxed...

breathe out, feel calm...
Breathe in, feel relaxed...
breathe out, feel calm...
The liquid sunlight is filling every inch of your body and is taking away all the anxiety and stress of the day. Keep breathing, I will give you a few more minutes to stay in this state as the liquid sunlight is purifying your body and soul.
Breathe in, feel relaxed...
breathe out, feel calm...
Breathe in, feel relaxed...
breathe out, feel calm...
Breathe in, feel relaxed...
breathe out, feel calm...
Breathe in, feel relaxed...
breathe out, feel calm...
Breathe in, feel relaxed...
breathe out, feel calm...
Breathe in, feel relaxed...
breathe out, feel calm...
Breathe in, feel relaxed...
breathe out, feel calm...
Breathe in, feel relaxed...
breathe out, feel calm...
Breathe in, feel relaxed...

breathe out, feel calm...
Breathe in, feel relaxed...
breathe out, feel calm...
Breathe in, feel relaxed...
breathe out, feel calm...
Breathe in, feel relaxed...
breathe out, feel calm...
Breathe in, feel relaxed...
breathe out, feel calm...
Breathe in, feel relaxed...
breathe out, feel calm...
Breathe in, feel relaxed...
breathe out, feel calm...
Breathe in, feel relaxed...
breathe out, feel calm...

As the light comes down your body, feel your body being filled not only with the warm liquid, but with positive and loving thoughts as well.

Focus your attention on everything good that is going on in the world. The fact that you are alive and breathing is a miracle in itself, so acknowledge it inside your mind. Picture something that makes you happy and that resembles positive energy in your life.

Personally, I like to picture a beautiful white flower, but you can choose whatever fits your soul the best. Just paint it in your mind and breathe into it.
Breathe in, feel relaxed...
breathe out, feel calm...
Breathe in, feel relaxed...
breathe out, feel calm...
Breathe in, feel relaxed...
breathe out, feel calm...
Breathe in, feel relaxed...
breathe out, feel calm...
Having a clear image is key, as it will allow you to take it with you during the rest of the entire day. So, I will give you all the time you need.
Breathe in, feel relaxed...
breathe out, feel calm...
Breathe in, feel relaxed...
breathe out, feel calm...
Breathe in, feel relaxed...
breathe out, feel calm...
Breathe in, feel relaxed...
breathe out, feel calm...
Breathe in, feel relaxed...
breathe out, feel calm...

Breathe in, feel relaxed...
breathe out, feel calm...
Breathe in, feel relaxed...
breathe out, feel calm...
Breathe in, feel relaxed...
breathe out, feel calm...
Breathe in, feel relaxed...
breathe out, feel calm...
Breathe in, feel relaxed...
breathe out, feel calm...
Breathe in, feel relaxed...
breathe out, feel calm...
Breathe in, feel relaxed...
breathe out, feel calm...
Now bring the attention back to the body and start feeling your arms and legs once again. You can close your hands or move your fingers, just to take control of the space around you.

Please, keep the eyes closed for now and enjoy the beautiful moment you are living. You have given yourself the time to feel better and that is absolutely incredible.

Breathe in, feel relaxed...
breathe out, feel calm...
Breathe in, feel relaxed...

breathe out, feel calm...
Breathe in, feel relaxed...
breathe out, feel calm...
Breathe in, feel relaxed...
breathe out, feel calm...
Now become aware of the environment around you once again. Feel the different sounds, the temperature of the room you are in and once you are ready, open the eyes again.

Chapter 4: Guided Meditations For Letting Go Fear

There are two kinds of fear, deluded or unhealthy and non-deluded or healthy. These can likewise be separated into fear of the inescapable and fear of the evitable. The way to managing fear is to check which kind of fear we have and to change our unfortunate fears of what we can fail to address into solid, fitting fears of what we can take care of. We would then be able to utilize these as the inspiration to create asylum and to beat what is extremely risky, and even in the long run to defeat what at present appears to be unavoidable, for example, infection, seniority, and demise.

Changing Fear

When we are terrified, we ought to ask ourselves what we are really scared of. Is it accurate to say that we are terrified of becoming ill? In any case, at present we must choose between limited options in that, thus that fear is not useful. It is more astute to fear debased resurrection and the four streams of birth, maturing, infection, and passing, all brought about by our dreams. This fear is valuable; it is designated "renunciation", the desire certainly to escape from samsara's sufferings, the inspiration that will empower us to escape from samsara and all disorder.

Fear of Death

Then again, perhaps we are apprehensive about death. Once more, however, as we are certainly going to bite the dust, that fear is not helpful and will prompt wrong reactions, for example, disavowal or a feeling of worthlessness or unimportance in our life. Nonetheless, despite the fact that we need to bite the dust, we do not need to kick the bucket with an uncontrolled personality. It is hence insightful to change our fear of passing on into a fear of kicking the bucket with an uncontrolled personality, the inspiration that will guarantee we plan for a serene and controlled demise.

Maybe it is the fear of individuals loathing us.
Alter our perspective and like them.

Fear of Rejection

Then again, perhaps we fear dismissal. Once more, from where does this fear really stem? Maybe it is the fear of individuals hating us. So what would we be able to do about that? Alter our perspective and like them. That is in our control.

Fear of Being Caught

Our fear of duty, of being caught, not ready to retreat, can likewise be changed into a helpful fear when we perceive that what is truly catching us is our very own psyche. Genuine and solid fear originates from perceiving that we are not dedicated to our departure from samsara and fills in as the inspiration for looking for that pledge to getaway.

Freedom from Fear

As it were, we cannot control whether things will go our direction or not, however, we can figure out how to control our very own personalities, our reactions, and our very own lead, and along these lines systematically locate certified freedom from all fear. As Shantideva says in Manual for the Bodhisattva's Lifestyle:

The wellspring of all our fear originates from our own uncontrolled personalities or "dreams".

There are fears that emerge from connection, for example, the fear and nervousness of not finding or being isolated from a person or thing we believe we require for our security or satisfaction.

There are fears that emerge from annoyance and contempt. A few fears are legitimately relative to our sentiment of being undermined by others, which is the reason we blow up and rationally or physically attempt to push the individual away.

What's more, specifically, there are fears that emerge from the psyche of self-getting a handle on obliviousness, which is the base of every single other daydream, and in this manner the wellspring all things considered.

To conquer this foundation of all fear, Buddha showed the reality of void or no-self.

The Root of All Fear

Self-getting a handle on is a numbness of the manner in which things are, a mind that grips at ourselves and our general surroundings as genuine, innately existent, existing out there free of the brain, having nothing to do with our seeing awareness. To beat this foundation of all fear, Buddha showed the reality of vacancy or no-self. This is a significant subject, yet we can increase some comprehension by thinking about our fantasies.

Much the same as a Fantasy

Similarly as all the fear, risk, and enduring we involve in a bad dream originates from not understanding that we are just envisioning, so all the fear and enduring we experience during our life originates from not seeing the genuine idea of our reality and our experience. The world does not exist independently from the psyche. Our conviction that things exist "out there", free of our brain, is the wellspring of all our fear. When we see straightforwardly that everything is anticipated by our seeing mindfulness, similar to the items in a fantasy, every one of our fears and issues will vanish. We endure in light of the fact that we are sleeping and lost in our fantasies, and we will quit enduring just when we wake up and consider things to be they truly are. The motivation behind the entirety of Buddha's lessons is to enable us to wake up.

In spite of the fact that things show up as strong, genuine, and free of the psyche, in all actuality they are as deficient as a fantasy.

Assume that last night we envisioned a tiger was pursuing us. While we were imagining, the tiger seemed all-around distinctively to exist from its very own side, which is the reason we created fear and fled from it. We felt emphatically we were being pursued by a genuine tiger and had no feeling that the tiger was simply and appearance to our brain. However, when we woke up, we understood that the tiger was just our very own projection mind-it did not exist from its very own side, in our little room! We quickly understood our mix-up and saw that the tiger was just our very own projection mind, thus our fear died down.

Mere Appearance to Mind

The tiger stopped when the fantasy psyche stopped. The equivalent is valid for the world we experience while we are wakeful. In spite of the fact that it shows up as strong, genuine, and free of the psyche, as a general rule it is as meager as a fantasy. Fantasy is a mixed-up appearance to mind that emerges from rest. It is confused on the grounds that with as long as we are imagining, the fantasy world seems to exist from their own side, free of our brain, while in truth it is a simple appearance to mind. Precisely the equivalent, in any case, is valid for the world we experience while we are wakeful. In spite of the fact that things show up as strong, genuine, and free of the psyche, in all actuality, they are as inadequate as a fantasy.

We are tricked totally by appearances – not for a minute do we question their legitimacy.

Sleep of Ignorance

Everything in samsara – our bodies, satisfactions, and the universes we occupy – are much the same as the things found in a fantasy. They are mixed up appearances emerging from the rest of numbness. Things dishonestly seem to exist from their very own side, outside the psyche, and we are totally taken in by their appearance. At the point when a disagreeable item, for example, a foe appears to our psyche, we fully trust this appearance as a genuine, remotely existent foe, thus we respond with fear or threatening vibe; and when an appealing article, for example, an excellent man or lady appears to our mind we are similarly taken in and react with envious connection. We are tricked totally by appearances – not for a minute do we question their legitimacy. On the off chance that we questioned appearances, we would find that that is all they are:

simple appearances to mind, with no genuine article behind them. The foe we battle or escape from is not any more genuine than the tiger in the fantasy and has no more capacity to hurt what we truly are. Also, the excellent man or lady we are so joined to resembles a sweetheart we meet in a fantasy, a simple appearance emerging like a wave in the sea of our psyche and later dissolving back once more.

How Thought Purges The Mind Of Fears and Phobias

"Phobia" is one of the different words that our general populace abuses and misuses. At whatever point somebody fears something, we state he has a phobia; in any case, this is not normally the situation. Phobias are the totally genuine mental issue that oppositely impact the individual's life; anyway, fear and weight can be sound and target reactions to speedy advancing toward danger. An awareness of this capability is one key to seeing how reflection benefits the individuals who experience the malicious effects of veritable phobias.

Fear and uneasiness can end up senseless and demolishing due to an update that the mind frill with peril and negativity. In case an individual was affirmed in the basement as a tyke, for example, she may have a fear of encased spaces, or claustrophobia. Despite how her fear was sound and reasonable at the season of the abuse, as her body was pushing her to escape or fight the unsafe condition, it is horrible and amazing when she concretes at accepting harmless to space as an adult. This kind of frenzy frequently feels wild to the individual who encounters it. Their heart starts to race, their breathing rate goes higher, and they may feel as though they are hyperventilating while the silence and recollections identified with the underlying upgrade flood her mind. This dreadful response comes from the amygdala, which is a notice framework in the cerebrum that starts the "battle or flight" reaction. The considerations that she has about her present condition of being, for example, "I am apprehensive," originate from the ventrolateral prefrontal cortex, which uses words to name and translates feeling.

The association between the amygdala and the ventrolateral prefrontal cortex is the spot reflection's ability abides for the people who experience the evil impacts of fears. As an individual transforms their situation into words and checks, activity in her amygdala lessens. This decrease in amygdalae development diminishes or turns away the reactions of free for all that they would typically have in light of the improvement, and it is with the thought that they make sense of how to purposely process a condition accordingly.

Meditation enables you to perceive musings and sentiments without having a passionate response to them. You center around a positive word or on a quieting scene in your psyche, and after that sit as a disconnected onlooker to your own brain and body. At the point when some other idea or sensation goes through you, you mark it as opposed to reacting to it.

Routine with regards to meditation likewise prepares your brain to embrace the here and now. Fears originate from past occasions, and tension is frequently a reaction to dread of the quick or inaccessible future. When you center around the present—or live in the now—your amygdala experiences fewer motivations to enact.

In the event that the individual with claustrophobia was to rehearse this normally, they could figure out how to promptly watch her enthusiastic and physical responses with words, for example, "sweat-soaked palms" and "sentiments of dread," and afterward enable them to proceed by not distracting their psyche. Also, as they reinforce their capacity and inclination to concentrate on the present, they improve their capacity to remain before initiating boosts without partnering it with a negative past occasion. The constant routine with regards to contemplation causes you to process nonsensical feelings of trepidation and regular daily existence through the ventrolateral prefrontal cortex, which, thus, can lessen or even anticipate the beginning of troubling enthusiastic reactions. As the phobic individual improves her capacity to think and steadily opens herself to the object of dread, she shows her amygdala to react just as required.

Letting Go of Fear Meditations

QIGONG MEDITATION

In customary Chinese medicine, it is accepted that fear is put away in the kidneys. In the western world, it is realized that frightful musings are minimal more than substance and electrical sign, activated through a perplexing system of correspondence in the body's cells. With enough redundancy, those neural pathways are framed and solidified, causing a similar reaction each time a risk is identified.

At the point when the psyche is looked with risk, regardless of whether genuine or not, it revisits those pathways to do similar activities. Furthermore, that is the place qigong reflection ventures in. By repeating positive musings, you can make and fortify neural pathways, and clear up the kidneys, to assist you with more prominent authority over your feelings.

Try it yourself:

Sit with your shoulders loose and your feet level against the floor. Spot your hands over your kidneys at your back under your lower ribs. Picture them and the little adrenal organs over them in your psyche.

Closer your eyes, grin, and breath in your stomach out, envisioning dim blue light and harmony encompassing your kidneys and adrenal organs. Breathe out by driving your stomach back in.

LEAN IN

The act of meditation is intended to be commonsense—helping us travel during our time with a touchstone of harmony and care. Similarly, as with any feeling, meditation can help settle us despite dread to enable us to comprehend it all the more obviously.

As the day progressed, you can enable yourself to meet fear in a progressively positive manner with the intensity of meditation.

Try it yourself:

Check-in with your emotions reliably. At whatever point you feel repulsive, let the tendency remain.

As opposed to running, embrace a full breath and technique your thoughts of dread and worry with warmth and intrigue. Be minding to yourself in fear, as you would for a trusted sidekick.

If you have adequate vitality and space, plunk down and breathe in into your fear for ten breath cycles.

FEAR AS POWER

Chris Bertish is a world-record-holding huge wave surfer. What's more, he has intriguing things to state about dread:

"Fear is stating: this is the ideal time to have the option to do what you're attempting to do. Your body is really setting you up to have a positive result. When you can truly comprehend that fear is a feeling like some other feeling, you can figure out how to oversee it. And after that, you can do things that a great many people consider to be uncommon."

Bertish has figured out how to oversee and process his dread to make it work for him, enabling it to help him to mind-boggling accomplishments of solidarity.

Try it yourself:

To beat my fear of heights, I have grasped the fear, taking a lead rock climbing class where I need to move to the highest point of the divider and free fall mostly down the divider before being securely grabbed with a rope.

Through training, receptiveness, and cheering companions and teachers, I have figured out how to inhale through the dread and let go repeatedly. The fear remains, however my response to it has changed.

Did you practice it yourself? — What is your fear? What little, safe advances would you be able to take to work on disapproving of your breath in that fear? As you practice, what changes do you see after some time?

A Simple Visualization

We can attempt this following basic perception to relinquish fear and uneasiness. Sitting in an agreeable position for contemplation, with a straight back, we close our eyes and inhale normally through our nose. At that point, we invest a little energy recognizing what it is we are at present scared of. We recognize our tricked, undesirable fears, for example, the fear of passing on, the fear of misfortune, the fear of disappointment, etc. Utilizing our intelligence, we comprehend that every one of these fears, and all threats, emerge on account of our betrayed personalities and antagonistic activities.

We can then be able to see the fears as one along with their causes, personalities that are negative and their activities as a thick cloud of smoke, as we exhale it. This bad smoke then dissipates and eventually disappears. As you take a breath, try to envision that you are absorbing all of the surrounding fearlessness and vitality of everything that is made of white light and fills up our psyche and body.

After we do this a few times, we begin to feel both our brain and body become completely free and have received all that we requested and feel very secure and blessed among others. We feel our body being supple and with a clear, fearless, and tranquil mind.

Then, let the feeling slowly escape from deep within and allow it to fill up your entire aura and body.

Then give thanks for the help you received during a difficult time.

Keep in mind that we have an unrestrained choice. Soul regards us through and through freedom, thus we have to request help when required.

At whatever point you are feeling on edge or fearful, make sure to rehearse this reflection. After some time, your fears will turn out to be less and increasingly reasonable, yet it requires exertion and practice.

Chapter 5: Third Week Of Meditations

As we move into our third week of meditation practice, you may notice that our final week of meditation exercises revolve solely around personal development issues. Previously in the first week you were acquainted with various forms of self-care and self-betterment, while in the second week of meditations you were taught how to focus your attention on advanced meditation techniques that would help you to use meditation as a tool. In this final week of meditations, you are provided with 7 basic meditative processes, including micro-focusing, mindfulness, combating procrastination, deep screen, and positive thinking. The final seven meditational techniques are designed to help you develop specific skills so that you can enhance the quality of your life through meditation.

15. Micro Focusing Meditation

For starters we will be dealing with micro focusing, which is a form of meditation where individuals use moments of awareness to help enhance their ability to concentrate and focus. The type of micro focusing that we will be dealing with in today's meditation, focuses primarily with momentary mindfulness in terms of office atmospheres and limited time slots.

You'll notice that there are many people who claim they want to practice meditation and then point out the are unable to do so because they can't seem to find enough time. Now, while in order to get the best results it is important that we use full-bodied meditational programs, it is actually possible to use moments of mindfulness in an office setting to induce calm and enhance awareness. This specific form of short-term awareness enhancing is known as micro focusing.

In order to begin your micro focusing meditation, you will first need to find yourself a calm, quiet place where you can dedicate 5 to 10 minutes of absolute silence. This can be difficult when there are other people around, like in an office environment. But, you might be able to steal away a few minutes of private time in a stairwell, in the bathroom, or in an empty office space. Once you have decided on a specific location, get yourself into a meditative posture, generally a seated chair posture, and clear your mind by drawing in a deep breath.

You are now ready to begin your micro focusing meditation.

Draw a deep clear breath into your body and then slowly to the count of five begin to release.

1.
2.
3.
4.
5.

Breathe in.
Hold.
Relax.
Release.
And repeat -
Breathe in.
Hold.

Relax.
Release.
And again, breathe in.
Hold.
One.
Two.
Three.
Four.
Five.
Relax.
Release.
You are in this moment surrounded by light.
Breathe in.
Hold.
Relax.
Release.
Your mind is like a sword.
On its own, it has the ability to cut through problems. Its ability to effectively do so however it depends on how well your mind is maintained.
Just as a sword must be honed. Your mind also needs to be effectively honed and taken care of.
Breathe in.

Hold.
One.
Two.
Three.
Four.
Five.
Relax.
Release.
To do so you need to teach yourself how to focus on the minute details in your life.
Remember, you are full of positive energy. It is your job to use that positive energy to generate positive actions.
Breathe in.
Hold.
One.
Two.
Three.
Four.
Five.
Relax.
Release.
As you are assigned tasks throughout the day it is your job to bring your mind back from the distractions you face.
Breathe in.

Hold.
Relax.
Release.
If you see something that demands you immediate attention, you must find the strength to focus on the task and get it done regardless of what might distract you.
You are strong minded.
Distractions cannot control you.
Breathe in.
Hold.
Relax.
Release.
As you move forward with your day, you will find that the more effective you are with each individual task – the quicker you are able to indulge yourself.
Breathe in.
Hold.
Relax.
Release.
You are ready to bring your mind back to focus on your tasks at hand.
Bonus Affirmations

I'm focused and resourceful. My inner vision is clear and uncluttered. My ability to see and focus my power is what enables me to change my life.

I consciously choose to allow my clarity of mind impact my daily life. It is with this clarity that I choose to live a healthier, organized life.

I'm dynamic and full of energy. My energy comes from the fact that I do not waste time or talent on clutter. I organize my mind to teach myself to focus clearly on one specific task at a time.

I find it easy to focus on key tasks. The ability to control my mind is something that comes naturally to me.

My mind is a tool that allows me to constantly come up with brilliant ideas. My ability to create new things is what allows me to craft more opportunities for myself.

My mind always thinks of healthy, and positive thoughts. The positivity that I have ingrained in my mind is what allows it to constantly stay open and focused at the same time.

My memory is outstanding. Because of how good my memory I find it extremely easy to tackle new challenges by drawing inspiration from past events.

I'm a fast learner. My ability to learn things quickly comes from the fact that my mind effortlessly focuses on the key points of any discussion.

My mind is strange focus on the positives. By training my mind to focus on the positives I shield it from negativity.

I'm creative, smart and intelligent. My ability to focus on minute details and varied topics allows me to maintain my intelligence levels.

16. Mindfulness Meditation

The next form of meditation that you will be learning is mindfulness meditation. Mindfulness meditation refers to a form of mental training where you get your mind to focus on specific experiences by way of highlighting your personal emotions, your thought process and how you felt throughout the experience. This will help you develop a better understanding of yourself and the experiences that you have gone through. This type of meditation is known to reduce stress, and has been used to treat multiple health conditions including chronic pain, insomnia and depression.

To begin your mindfulness meditation, select a quiet and comfortable spot where you be undisturbed for the next 10 to 30 minutes. Keep in mind that mindfulness meditation is best practiced outdoors where you can feel the fresh air against your skin. If however you are not able to do so, try to find a spot that has sunlight or open windows, as this will allow you to develop a closer connection with your surroundings. Once you are seated, draw a deep breath as you close your eyes.

You are now ready to begin your mindful meditation.

Draw a deep clear breath into your body, and then slowly to the count of five begin to release.

Breathe in.

Hold.

Relax.

Release.

And repeat -
Breathe in.
Hold.
Relax.
Release.
And again, breathe in.
Hold.
Relax.
Release.
You are in this moment surrounded by light.
Breathe in.
Hold.
Relax.
Release.
As you focus your mind you will notice that the external noises around you have begun to slowly dissipate.
You are a mindful person. You have the ability to slowly bring your focus to one single point. For you that one single point is the air that is blowing in and out of your body.
Breathe in.
Hold.
Relax.

Release.
Everything else around you is standing still.
You are energy.
Your energy is filling your entire being and allowing your mind to come alive.
Breathe in.
Hold.
Relax.
Release.
And now, as you adjust yourself to a more comfortable position, say to yourself -
I am mindful.
My mindfulness comes from my efforts to consciously choose stillness and happiness.
I am content and complete.
Breathe in.
Hold.
Relax.
Release.
In this moment, I am awake.
I am consciously picking through the clutter of my mind and organizing it into labeled boxes and folders so that my mind's energy can freely move around me.

Breathe in.
Hold.
Relax.
Release.
As you continue to move through your mind your body has now become physically lighter.
Breathe in.
Hold.
Relax.
Release.
You are no longer weighed down by the weight of unwanted distractions. Your mind is clear and mindful.

Bonus Affirmations

I am fearless. My self-confidence is built on the fact that I refuse to cower under any circumstances.

I'm unique and so are my thoughts. Because I respect my mind and the thoughts that it generates, my mind in turn allows me to become a more fulfilled individual.

I am talented and intelligent. My ability to love myself from my talent has shown me that positivity brings me further than negativity does.

I am mindful of my time and I refuse to waste it on things that are outside of my control. My time is valuable.

I am mindful of my efforts, and I refuse to give up after I fail just one time because I know that failure is a stepping stone to success.

I consciously choose to create happiness and love in my life. Because of this choice I'm able to love and accept myself for who I am and who I want to be.

I trust myself and I trust my ability to do better today than I did yesterday. I'm constantly trying to be better and better each and every day of my life.

I am a collection of many things - I'm trusting and bright, I am calm and adventurous, I am transformed and complete.

I mindfully choose to be fully present in the now, I make this choice because I do not believe the next moment is more important than the moment that I am currently in.

I am aware of what is happening to me in this current moment and I cannot wish it to be any different. Every moment for me is a journey that shapes and molds me into the best version of myself.

17. Universal Breath Meditation

The next form of meditation that we will try is the universal breath. This is an extremely advanced form of meditation. Meditation cleaning is generally used as a technique to induce calm. In truth, however meditation, is actually induced by breathing itself. This is because breath awareness itself can be a form of meditative insight. Every breath you take draws into your body oxygen that is being given off as excess by the plants and trees around you. At the same time, the carbon dioxide that you are releasing from your body is actually being drawn by plants as their form of "oxygen." In this way, everything in the universe cycles around. Everything that you produce, just be living and breathing, is given to another and everything that you retain comes from another. Breath awareness meditation allows you to identify this universal form of unity that exists between all living creatures.

Universal breath meditation must be conducted in the open air. Find a rooftop, balcony, quiet spot in a park or any appropriate outside environment that would be conducive to the practice. Position yourself in your posture of choice. Once you feel comfortable, close your eyes and draw in a deep breath, and then exhale. Repeat the process three more times.

You are now ready to begin your universal breath meditation.

As you close your eyes carefully is important for you to slowly even out your breathing so that you can count exactly how long it takes every breath of air into the body to travel through it and then slowly to expel itself.

Breathe in.

Relax.

Release.

Breathe in deeply, again.

Relax.

And release.

Each breath that you draw into your own body is a breath of air that has come to you from the universe itself. There is no difference between you and the universe. You are a part of the universe and the universe is a part of you.

Breathe in.

Relax.

Release.

Breathe in deeply, again.

Relax.

And release

Today in this moment you are reminding yourself of how the universe is part of your life.

As a positive asset, it is your job to allow positive energy to flow from you into the universe.

At the same time, it is also important positive energy to flow from the universe into you.

You are part of the universe, and you are constantly allowing it to grow.

Breathe.

Hold.

One.
Two.
Three.
Four.
Relax.
The universe has no demands from you.
The universe does not seek to take things away.
The universe always seeks to give, and bestow upon you the most positive of emotions.
Breathe in.
Relax.
Release.
Breathe in deeply, again.
Relax.
And release
Your life has purpose because you are part of the universe. You are a child of the universe, and the universe seeks to take care of you.
Breathe in deeply, and open your eyes.
Bonus Affirmations
Today I am choosing to effectively communicate with the universe. The

universe is a part of me and I am part of the universe.

Today in this moment, I am accepting the energy that the universe is sending to me. I am the vessel and the energy that I store inside myself is a mere part of the energy that the universe retains within it.

I am a positive asset to the universe. My positive energy allows the universe to grow and bloom.

The universe accepts me and loves me for who I am, including my flaws and mistakes.

The universe is not my enemy – whenever the universe gives me a challenge it also gives me an opportunity to overcome it.

The universe showers me with love and abundance. The immense part of energy that the universe generates and supports me with has allowed me to become a better version of myself.

I am one with the universe. There is no distinct line that distinguishes where I begin and where the universe ends.

I allow the universe to love and take care of me. The universe chooses to protect me and love me because I am an extension of it.

I am a magnet for positive energy. Positive energy comes to me in waves, while negative energy is repelled by me.

I have faith in the universe because the universe has been there to support me through all my trials and tribulations.

18. Positive Thinking Meditation

The next form of meditative mindfulness that we will be practicing deals with positive thinking. Sometimes the notion of "positive thinking" is thought of as a "fluff" term. We are all encouraged to think positively and in a state of mind that focuses on happiness. However, positive thinking is a powerful tool, and an advanced meditative process that trains the mind to exclude negative emotions and perceptions, and build up positive thoughts and focus by enhancing mindfulness.

On a more practical level positive mindfulness allows individuals to look forward to challenges and obstacles instead of being afraid of them. Imagine that you have an upcoming interview. Instead of feeling anxious about whether or not you will do well, if you can change your energy, and encourage yourself to feel happier and more excited than you feel insecure, odds are you will actually do much better in the interview.

Positive thinking meditation is also generally practiced in an open, outdoor area. However, if you find it difficult to find a spot outdoors, try waking up very early and practice it in first light, on your bed. Fortunately, positive thinking meditation does not provide a specific posture so you can literally practice it anywhere you want. It is advisable that you practice this particular meditation at least twice a month in order to maximize its effect.

Once you have found yourself a comfortable spot, draw in a deep breath and begin.

You are now ready to begin your positive thinking meditation.

Begin by very carefully breathing in and allowing your mind to enter a relaxed state of being.
Breathe in.
Relax.
Release.
Breathe in deeply, again.
Relax.
And release.
As you continue to focus your attention on your breathing, remind yourself of who you want to be as a person.
As an individual you have been strong, and courageous.
Your courage comes from your ability to take on any task with a clear and positive mind-set.
You are a brave and capable, and you are not afraid to get your work done.
Breathe in.
Relax.
Release.
Breathe in deeply, again.
Relax.
And release

You are important, and your importance is such that each of these tasks must be addressed by you.

But most importantly, you are needed and acknowledged, so as your workload increases you are also rewarded in multiple ways as you complete your tasks.

Breathe.

Hold.

Relax.

Start to tap into the positivity that you have. Bring your focus on to your current tasks. From this moment on you will look to each task, and consider them to be an extension of a greater positive goal that you have set for yourself.

Breathe in.

Relax.

Release.

Breathe in deeply, again.

Relax.

And release

Everything you do has a purpose, and you are able to execute these things because you have courage and belief in yourself.

You are significant.

You are not disposable.
You are needed.
You are loved.
Breathe in.
Relax.
Release.
Breathe in deeply, again.
Relax.
And release

By reminding yourself of the love that other people have for you, you are reminding yourself of your purpose in life and the things you have to be grateful for.

You are content.
You are able.
You are whole.
Breathe in.
Relax.
Release.
Breathe in deeply, again.
Relax.

Your positive mind and spirit allows you to do all that is required of you.

Breathe in deeply and slowly, then open your eyes.

Bonus Affirmations

I am a positive person who strongly believes in my own skills and abilities. My positivity is what allows me to constantly learn and grow so much so that my growth is endless.

Because I am a positive person I understand that mistakes are not problems, but rather that they are in opportunity to succeed.

I'm smart and intelligent, my intelligence is such that I have great ideas that I believe will make useful contributions to society.

I am a strong individual. My strength comes from the understanding that I am the best version of myself and that every single day I need to choose to be a better version of myself.

I'm a kind and beautiful person. I believe that beauty comes not from external appearances but an understanding of one's own self-worth.

I make a conscious effort to be kinder to the people that I work with. I believe that kindness is what makes the universe go around. I know that when I am kind to people, the universe will be kinder to me.

I am a work in progress. Even though I am not yet the person that I aspire to be I am constantly taking steps to be the best version of myself and to be a better version than I was yesterday.

Because I'm a positive individual, I give myself permission to be strong and happy at the same time. Being happy does not mean that I'm weak, it means that I'm strong enough to overcome my obstacles and be positive minded.

Insecurities and fear cannot control me. Because I'm a positive individual who chooses to pursue joy, insecurities and fear simply pass me by.

Negativity does not speak to me. I'm not attracted by the negative patterns of speech, instead I believe that positivity and gratitude have more to offer.

19. Procrastination Meditation

The next form of meditation that we will be learning is known as procrastination meditation. Because the world we live in is so full of various forms of distraction, it is common for individuals to find it difficult to focus on specific topics. The inability to concentrate has actually been enhanced due to the nature of social media, and technological dependency that has developed in the last 10 to 15 years. Individuals who have difficulty carrying through assigned tasks often find that these distractions play a major role in terms of how they deal with obligations and duties assigned to them. The best way to deal with distractions is to use meditative techniques to help enhance your concentration. With more focus, you are less likely to procrastinate and, as a result, you will be more productive and efficient.

Procrastination meditation, much like positive thinking meditation, does not need to be performed outdoors. In fact, procrastination meditation can be practiced just about anywhere.

Once you have found yourself in a comfortable position, simply close your eyes and draw in a deep breath.

You are now ready to begin your procrastination meditation.

As you begin your meditative session keep in mind that your key point today is to remind yourself of the importance of completing your tasks on time.
Slowly, release your breath to the count of four.
Hold.
Now as you draw in your breath again, draw in the breath four seconds at a time, and hold, and release.
Repeat this exercise four more times.
Breathe in.
Hold.
Release.
Breathe in.
Hold.
Release.
Breathe in.
Hold.
Release.
Breathe in.
Hold.
Release.
As you focus carefully on your breathing, remind yourself of the goals that you have

set for yourself today. Why is it important for you to complete these tasks today?
Breathe in.
Hold.
Release.
Ask yourself, who it is you want to be, and as you do repeat to yourself why it is you need to complete your tasks.
Breathe in.
Hold.
Release.
You are strong and capable.
As a strong capable individual, you are the only person who can complete the tasks that you have been assigned.
You are strong and positive and your positivity is what will allow you to take responsibility for your tasks and to move forward with them.
You are powerful.
You are capable.
Now, say to yourself -
I am responsible for my own life.
I am capable of taking care of my own tasks.
Breathe in.

Hold.
Release.
I am committed to my own personal growth.
Breathe in.
Hold.
Release.
I am bringing my own abilities to the table and am choosing to use them to be a better version of myself.
Breathe in.
Hold.
Release.
There is nothing that I can't do.
Breathe in.
Hold.
Release.
Breathe in.
I am now ready to face my daily tasks.
Breathe in.
Hold.
Release.
Slowly open your eyes.
Bonus Affirmations
I consciously choose to decide my own fate. I plan out my day and I ensure that I

stick to my schedule. If not, I find that my day will get away from me.

In order to overcome procrastination, I find it important to take charge and get things done right now. By delaying tasks, I ultimately delete tasks.

In order to prevent myself from procrastinating I consciously move forward with my goals. I'm not allowed to indulge myself until I have achieved the target goal I have set for myself.

I'm someone who seizes the moment, and I seize the moment by constantly taking action instead of allowing minor setbacks to hold me back.

I am successful because I have an amazing work ethic. My work ethic is what has allowed me to succeed in life.

I'm not afraid of failure. Small failures do not deter me from my path; they merely encourage me to go on and go forward, because I know that until and unless I'm constantly moving forward, I will not be able to reach my goals.

I am a do-er not a wait-er. By constantly ensuring that I am doing when I'm supposed to, I ensure that I don't have to wait upon other people to help me.

Procrastination is a form of fear of getting things done and I am a strong individual who is not afraid of getting things done.

When I work, I work with abundant enthusiasm and confidence. I'm confident about my work because I put my hundred percent in it.

My life is an adventure that is waiting to be lived out, by delaying living I'm delaying myself an opportunity be truly alive.

20. Conscious Resistance Meditation

This form of meditation that we will be learning allows individuals to combat conscious resistance. Conscious resistance is an issue that people under the age of 30 and above the age of 45 tend to deal with quite a lot. This is understandable, because no one really likes to be told what they can and can't do. The problem with this is that by convincing yourself that you should do something, or convincing someone else that they should do something every single time you need a task completed, isn't only be tedious, it can also be extremely time-consuming. Conscious resistance meditation trains your mind to understand that "following orders" is not necessarily a bad thing. Not only does this help enhance performance and office atmospheres, for example, it can actually help you get along better in a wide variety of social situations.

Start by finding yourself in a quiet corner where you will not be disturbed for the next 10 to 30 minutes, and then draw in a deep breath and slowly close your eyes.

You are now ready to begin your conscience resistance meditation.

As you slowly close your eyes, fix within your mind's eye a point from which you shall radiate your positive energy.

As we grow older, one of the major problems that we face is that we find it harder and harder to accept what other people have to say. Be it advice or suggestions.

Our ego builds itself to be larger than the opportunities that are offered to us.

Breathe in deeply.

Hold.

And release.

The reason egoism is able to take over our mind and form an invisible barrier is because we are afraid.

But as we go through this meditation today, we are going to teach ourselves how not to be afraid.

Breathe in slowly to the count of five.

Hold for four seconds.

And then slowly release.

Once again - Breathe in deeply.

Hold.

And release.

Today you will be given an opportunity to clear your mind of all these negative thoughts that have weaved their way into your consciousness.

And as we finish you will find that your mind is not only clearer, it is more receptive to help and suggestions.

Breathe in deeply.

Hold.

And release.

Remind yourself today of who you are.

You are a capable individual.

You are gifted.

Your talents have no limit.
You are confident and positive minded.
As a confident and positive person you find it easy to accept help and to follow directions when your work or life requires you to do so.
Following orders does not make you less of a person and you are not intimidated by directions.
Exhale deeply, and purge yourself of all the negative stress and energy that you have inside yourself.
As you do, remind yourself of the following -
You are capable.
You are intelligent.
You are efficient and worthy.
You are talented and resourceful.
As you remind yourself, allow your mind to channel your energy toward the tasks that you have been assigned.
You are capable.
You are intelligent.
You are efficient and worthy.
You are talented and resourceful.

Repeat the last four phrases in your mind once again.
You are capable.
You are intelligent.
You are efficient and worthy.
You are talented and resourceful.
Breathe in deeply.
Hold.
And release.
Breathe in deeply.
Hold.
And release.
Breathe in deeply.
Hold.
And release.
And relax. You are now ready to break through your conscious resistance.

Bonus Affirmations

I defeat resistance on a daily basis by changing what I am pushing away, into what I am trying to attract.

Resisting change is a waste of energy. Because I am a smart individual, I do not waste my energy on things that I cannot control.

The concept of resistance arises from a lack of ability to achieve what you want in life. I have achieved, and continue to achieve what I want in life and as such a resistant conscious or subconscious is not part of my personality.

I am fully capable of accepting orders without facing resistance from my own self.

I consciously choose to release resistance from my mind and my life. I do not approve of resistance without meaning and as such I refuse to allow it to enter my life's orbit.

Resistance as a form of egoism. I refuse to resist that which I know will help me become a better person.

I am not irritated when I'm told what I need to do. Instead I choose to actively take part in completing the task as efficiently as possible.

I'm constantly creating new reasons to be stronger and better. My growth is not deterred by an egoistic refusal to seek help.

I am strong and powerful enough to understand when I need help. I'm capable of asking for help without falling back on resistance.

I'm letting go of resistance and choosing to actively trust the universe. The universe is vast and it is allowing me to grow without doubt or fear.

21. Deep Sleep Meditation

The final form of meditation that you will be practicing as part of this guided collection deals with the topic of deep sleep. Individuals who suffer from stress and anxiety disorders have often found that meditation is useful in helping them to overcome insomnia or sleep-related problems. Deep sleep medications are specifically structured to help you carefully lull your mind to a less anxious state of being so that you can overcome any form of insomnia or stress related sleep disorder.

To begin your meditation, first find a comfortable bed where you can start the meditation in a safe environment. Keep in mind that this particular form of meditation is meant to be conducted while in bed, as it can induce sleep in a matter of moments. It is extremely dangerous to be listening to deep sleep meditation while operating any form of heavy machinery or any vehicle of any type.

Once you have found a position that you find comfortable, close your eyes and draw in a deep breath.

You are now ready to begin your deep sleep meditation.

As you close your eyes and relax into the comfort of your bed, clearly and deeply breathe in and start the process of purging your body of stress.

Breathe in.

And release.

Follow this process an additional three times, and as you breathe in, this time consciously hold your breath for a moment before allowing yourself to release.

Breathe in.

Hold.

And release.

Breathe in.

Hold.
And release.
Breathe in.
Hold.
And release.
Your objective today is simple. You are going to relearn how to sleep. Sleep has eluded you for the past few days because your body and mind have not been able to relax enough to recognize that it is time for them to take a break.
Breathe in.
Hold.
And release.
Today you are both the student and the teacher. Not only are you going to teach yourself how to sleep, you're also going to learn how important it is to allow your anxiety to slip away.
We will be counting backward from sixty, and by the time we reach zero. This entire minute has been designed to allow you to consciously destress and remove all negative thoughts from your mind.
Breathe in.
Hold.

And release.

Your negativity is what prevents you from being able to have a restful night and as such we will first start by detoxing your mind of that deep rooted negativity.

And now we begin.

Sixty.
Fifty -nine.
Fifty -eight.
Fifty -seven.
Fifty -six.
Fifty -five.
Fifty -four.
Fifty -three.
Fifty -two.
Fifty-one.
Fifty.
Forty-nine.
Forty-eight.
Forty-seven.
Forty-six.
Forty-five.
Forty-four.
Forty-three.
Forty-two.
Forty-one

As you start to feel the weight of your eyes, ask yourself what it is that you think causes you to have such a hard time going to sleep.
What is it specifically that is worrying you?
What can you do about it?
Forty.
Thirty-nine.
Thirty-eight.
Thirty-seven.
Thirty-six.
Thirty-five.
Thirty-four.
Thirty-three.
Thirty-two.
Thirty-one
Thirty.
Focus on your fears.
What would happen if they came to fruition?
Breathe in.
Hold.
And release.
Ask yourself and be honest, what is the absolute worst that can happen?

Now ask yourself how much of what is happening is within your control?
Are the problems that you face within your control?
What can you do about them?
Twenty-nine.
Twenty-eight.
Twenty-seven.
Twenty-six.
Twenty-five.
Twenty-four.
Twenty-three.
Twenty-two.
Twenty-one.
Twenty.
If you cannot do anything to change the outcome, what is the point of allowing what you cannot change to impact your present moment?
Breathe in.
Hold.
And release.
Breathe in.
Hold.
And release.
Breathe in.

Hold.
And release.
The objective today is to simply let go of that which you cannot change and to relax.
Breathe in.
Hold.
Release
And relax.
Breathe in.
Hold.
Release
And relax.
Nineteen.
Eighteen.
Seventeen.
Sixteen.
Fifteen.
Fourteen.
Thirteen.
Twelve.
Eleven.
Ten.
Breathe in.
Hold.
Release

And relax.
Today you are relaxing, and as you do you are about to slip into a deep sleep that will allow you to refresh your mind and body.
Breathe in.
Hold.
Release
And relax.
Breathe in.
Hold.
Release
And relax.
Nine.
Eight.
Seven.
Six.
Breathe in.
Hold.
Release
And relax.
Five.
Breathe in.
Hold.
Release
And relax.
Four.

Three.
Two.
One.
Relax.

Bonus Affirmations

I am full of joy and happiness and my joy and happiness are what allow me to sleep a deep sleep, without interruptions.

Today I release from my body all forms of fear, worry, anger and blame. As I lay down and relax, anxiety and stress lose their grip on my mind and on my soul

Today I choose to forgive all that has happened to me. I believe that what has happened has happened in a way that is best for the world. I let go of all feelings of resentment and upset.

I now give myself permission to fall into a deep sleep. The way that I allow myself to rest determines how fresh I am tomorrow and how productive my day will be.

Today in this moment, I'm allowing my mind to enter a place of deep and restful sleep. My deep and restful sleep allows me to lighten my worldly burden and instead become a stronger and more positive person.

Today I choose to express my gratefulness. I'm grateful not only for my life, but for the people who have taught me how to lead it.

Today I choose peace. As I close my eyes and rest, I choose peace. I enter a world without stress or anxiety, where only positive thoughts lift me up.

Today I choose to match my heartbeat with the universe. I am in this very moment in harmony with the universe itself.

I pray today that my sleep be peaceful. I promote peaceful sleep by allowing myself to dream dreams that are filled with positive and loving thoughts.

Today I congratulate myself for having tried hard and doing my best. All my efforts today did not happen in vain.

Chapter 6: The Importance Of Meditation

At the point when the subject of mindfulness comes up, there are individuals out there who, despite everything, envision that meditation is the space of free spirits who appreciate daydreaming on a woven grass tangle someplace. Yet, the truth of the matter is that there's nothing charm about care and mindfulness reflection. These life-changing practices have been around for centuries, and practically every mysterious way coordinates some type of them.

Even though it has its foundations in Buddhism, non-mainstream care reflection as rehearsed today is open to individuals all things considered and convictions. Notwithstanding its astonishing ubiquity, you may ponder, "However, for what reason should I reflect?" To start to answer this (legitimate) question, we give six intriguing realities about contemplation beneath.

A couple of realities you may not think about contemplation:

Reflection makes you more joyful

Individuals who think for the most part have more joyful existences than the individuals who don't. Reflection is known to improve the progression of productive contemplations and positive feelings. Indeed, even a couple of moments spent ruminating normally can have a major effect. Logical proof backings this case: broad examinations were directed on a gathering of Buddhist priests as they were pondering. The pre-frontal cortex of the priests' cerebrums (the part connected with joy) was seen as an additional dynamic.

Reflection encourages you oversee tension, stress, and misery

The transformative capability of contemplation shouldn't be thought little of. Studies directed at the University of Wisconsin demonstrated that contemplation effectsly affects the mind. For instance, specialists found that the piece of the mind that directs pressure and nervousness shrivels when contemplation is drilled reliably. By concentrating on second-by-second encounters, meditators are preparing the psyche to resist the urge to panic, even in upsetting circumstances. Alongside this, they additionally experience less nervousness altogether because of vulnerability about what's to come.

You needn't be a strict individual to ruminate

The Mindworks Meditation organizers are certain that reflection can profit everybody. It is past regulation: it's tied in with creating smoothness, rehearsing mindfulness and cleaning up the psyche. What's more, in spite of the fact that thought is a key part of most world religions, you don't need to be stick to a religion to rehearse reflection. This is uplifting news for the one out of five Americans who characterize themselves as "otherworldly yet not strict!" Also, in January 2018 the Pew Research Center distributed discoveries that show exactly how standard care contemplation has become in the US, paying little mind to strict association.

Contemplation benefits are practically prompt

The various medical advantages that outcome from reflection are another extraordinary motivation to receive the training. Certain advantages can begin making themselves felt rapidly after individuals begin sitting. A feeling of tranquility and genuine feelings of serenity are basic encounters, regardless of whether this inclination is temporary and unobtrusive. In an article distributed in Forbes on the web, lawyer Jeena Cho records six experimentally demonstrated advantages that you might not have been expecting, remembering a decrease for verifiable race and age predisposition.

A few people stress that reflection is having the contrary impact on the grounds that their psyches appear to be busier than at any other time. Our recommendation: stay with it, and keep your meetings short. Contemplation isn't tied in with cleaning the record of your brain clean, it's tied in with monitoring what shows up there. Also, you're a stride ahead: you're as of now seeing how bustling the psyche can be.

Contemplation encourages you nod off

A sleeping disorder is an alarming condition – everyone fears a restless night. Tragically, about 33% of the American populace experiences some type of lack of sleep, regardless of whether infrequent or incessant. In case you're one of those misfortunate people who gaze at the roof and tally sheep the entire night without any result, contemplation could possibly be an answer. An article in the Harvard Health Blog affirms that reflection triggers the unwinding reaction – which is the reason a few people really have the contrary issue: they nod off when they start to contemplate!

Reflection hones your memory

Aside from upgrading your satisfaction and improving your general prosperity, contemplation likewise enables your memory to remain sharp and your focus stay consistent. With care reflection, you train in staying mindful of the current second in a non-critical way. Thusly, interruptions are less and less inclined to clear you away. Only one more motivation behind why you ought to contemplate.

We can't envision that you despite everything need persuading, particularly in the wake of perusing the 6 reflection realities and models introduced previously. To kick you off and prop you up on your careful excursion, our Mindworks Meditation Courses offer guided contemplations, tips, and motivation.

Chapter 7: Sleep Scripts

Now that you are ready to fall asleep take a deep breath in. Exhale slowly and expel any tension that may have built up during the last few exercises.

As you settle in for sleep, you may begin to have thoughts about what you have done today or things you need to get done tomorrow. Take another deep breath and let those thoughts go with your next exhale. At this moment, all you need to do is clear your mind. Today is over and tomorrow will come whether you worry about it or not. For now, clear your mind so you can wake up strong and healthy for your duties tomorrow.

For now, I want you to draw your attention to your body. Where did you store your tension today? I invite you to focus your attention on the tension and let it go as we practiced earlier. Feel now where your body is relaxed. Take a few moments to appreciate the sense of relaxation your body is feeling at this moment and allow it to spread through your whole body from head to toes.

Before you drift off to bed, let's fill your mind with peaceful images. By promoting positive mental images, this will help you relax and can help avoid nightmares. As we begin, I would like you to visualize a place where you feel safe and comfortable. Take a few moments and imagine how the place would be.

When you have your safe place in mind, I would like you to start to relax your body again. In order to get rid of nightmares, you will need to release all tension from your body. When we are fearful, this can create tension in our body. Try to pay special attention to your shoulders, hands, back, neck, and jaw. Often times, these are areas where our tension can creep in.

If you feel any of these areas tensing up, focus your attention here. Breathe in…and breathe out…choose to relax and soften these areas. As you breathe, imagine the air bringing total relaxation to these areas and allow the tension to leave your body. I invite you to continue this pattern until your breathing becomes deep and slow again.

Notice now how your body has become more relaxed than it was before. Feel as your muscles sink into the bed as you relax further and deeper. Your jaw is becoming loose. Your mouth is resting, and your teeth are slightly apart. Now, your neck is relaxing, and your shoulders are falling away. Allow this to happen and let your muscles become soft.

I want you to return to your safe place. Imagine that this place is spacious, comfortable, and filled with a positive light. In this place, you have nothing to worry about, and you have all the time in the world to focus on yourself.

In this safe place, I want you to imagine the sun streaming in. The light fills you with warm and positive emotion. Thee are windows where you can see the beautiful nature outside. Your space can be wherever you want it to be. It can be by the mountains, by the ocean, or perhaps even on a golf course.

Return your focus back on your safe place. Imagine how warm and comfortable the room is. Walk over toward the comfortable bed and imagine how wonderful it feels to sink into the sheets. The sun is shining down on you, and you feel relaxed and warm. The bed is so soft around you, and you feel so at peace at this moment.

Notice now how these peaceful thoughts begin to fill your mind. They are filling your conscious and are clear. Any other thoughts you had before are drifting away. Your mind is falling into a positive place as you feel yourself drifting away. The space around you is safe and peaceful, and beautiful.

Any other thoughts you have at this moment, pass through your mind and drift off like clouds drifting by. Allow these thoughts to pass without judgment. There is no sense in dwelling on them when you are in such a safe place. All you have at this moment is peace and quiet.

Any time a worried thought arises, you turn your focus back to your safe place. In this location, you can get rid of any stress you may have on a daily basis. You are here to relax and enjoy this moment. There is nothing that can bother you. You are free from stress and responsibilities here.

When you are ready, you feel your body begin to drift off to sleep. You are beginning to slip deeper and deeper toward the land of dreams. As you feel your attention drift, you are becoming sleepier, but you chose to focus on counting with me. As we count, you will become more relaxed as each number passes through.

We will now take a few breaths, and then I will count from the number one to the number ten. As you relax, your mind will drift off to a deep and refreshing sleep. Ready?

Breathe in...one...two...three...and out...two...three.

Breathe in...one...two...three...and out...two...three.

Breathe in...one...two...three...and out...two...three.

Wonderful. Now, count slowly with me…one…bring your focus to the number one…

Two…you are feeling more relaxed…you are calm and peaceful…you are drifting deeper and deeper toward a wonderful night of rest.

Three…gently feel as all of the tension leaves your body. There is nothing but total relaxation filling your mind and your body. At this moment, your only focus is on quietly counting numbers with me.

Four…picture the number in your mind's eye. You are feeling even more relaxed and at peace. Your legs and arms are falling pleasantly heavy. You are so relaxed. Your body is ready for sleep.

Five…you are drifting deeper. The sleep begins to wash over you. You are at peace. You are safe. You are warm and comfortable.

Six…so relaxed…drifting off slowly…

Seven…your mind and body are completely at peace. You have not felt this calm in a while…

Eight...everything is pleasant. Your body feels heavy with sleep.

Nine...allow your mind to drift...everything is floating, and relaxing...your eyelids feel comfortable and heavy...your mind giving in to the thought of sleep.

Ten...you are completely relaxed, and at peace...soon, you will be drifting off to a deep and comfortable sleep.

Now that you are ready to sleep, I will now count from the number one to the number five. All I want you to do is listen gently to the words I am saying. When I say the number five, you will drift out of hypnosis and sleep comfortably through the night.

In the morning, you will wake up feeling well rested and stress-free. You have worked on many incredible skills during this session. You should be proud of the hard work you have put in. Now, it is time to sleep so you can wake up in the morning feeling refreshed.

Termination/Conclusion

Now that you are ready to fall asleep, I want you to send your focus to how heavy and warm your body feels. Feel how warm your hands are and allow that feeling to spread through your whole body.

Take a few moments to notice how heavy your eyelids are. As you continue to breathe gently, they become heavier and heavier. It feels wonderful to rest your eyes as they remain relaxed and closed. All of the tension you had earlier has left and drifted away without a care in the world. Each breath you take allows the tension to slip through your fingers and your toes. All that you have left at this moment is total relaxation.

Now, allow your mind to drift away. There is no need to focus or think in these final moments before you drift off to sleep. Your mind is relaxed. Your body is relaxed. Your whole body feels warm, soft, and totally relaxed.

Your body is sinking down…down…deeper and deeper…focus on your breath as you slip into a comfortable sleep…

One…

Two…

Three…

Four…

I want you to keep counting on your own now. Try to focus on the numbers as they pass through your mind. If you lose count, start at one again. All you need to do is keep counting. Allow your thoughts to drift and tun back to the numbers. It becomes a lot of effort because you are so tired. It is becoming harder and harder to focus. Your mind keeps drifting away as you fall asleep.

Gently bring your thoughts back and begin counting again. With each breath, try to count the numbers again.

One...

Two...

Three...

Four...

You are finding it hard to focus. All of the numbers are blending together. You are much too sleepy to count at this moment. You are drifting deeper, hardly able to keep your thoughts straight.

It is okay. Now, just relax and continue to breathe gently. There is no need to count any longer. Allow your mind to drift off to sleep. Surrender to the heaviness of sleep.

Allow yourself to slip back into your happy place. This place is quiet and peaceful. You feel safe and relaxed.

Now, your body begins to feel like a feather. Your body floats gently toward sleep. You drift back and forth, down further and further toward sleep. Soon, you will rest peacefully in your safe place. You are so sleepy and gently drifting.

Now, I am going to count from the number one to the number five. There is no need to count along with me. When I say the number five, you will drift off into a full night of sleep. Ready?

One...you are filled with total relaxation. Allow yourself to fall into this comfortable sleep.

Two...after this session, every muscle, and nerve in your body is completely relaxed. Your limbs are loose and limp. You feel wonderful from the top of your head to the tip of your toes. You are ready to fall asleep any moment now.

Three...you are feeling perfect in every way possible. You feel perfect physically.

You have worked through this session to help your body heal itself.

You are feeling perfect mentally. You have worked through your issues and let go of the stress you have been holding onto. You are feeling calm and relaxed. You allow yourself to be happy and completely serene at this moment.

Four...you are almost completely asleep right now. Any moment, you will drift off and sleep through the whole night.

You are completely relaxed. Now, you will allow yourself to fall asleep. You will experience a wonderful and deep sleep like you never have before in your life.

In the morning, you will wake up at the correct time. You will wake up feeling full of energy, relaxed, and fully rested. By getting a full night of sleep, you will be setting yourself up for success tomorrow. You will love yourself and practice your new positive thoughts. Remember to breathe through the stress and try to be your most authentic self.

Breathe in...breathe out...when I say the number five...you will slip out of hypnosis and sleep.

Have wonderful dreams and enjoy the journey.

Five.

Sleep Meditation

You would not believe how difficult sleep is nowadays.

Do you struggle to fall asleep at night? Do you toss and turn when you do try to fall asleep?

Do you feel exhausted the next day?

You are not alone! It is very common for the average person to be filled to the brim with stress. There is only so much time in the day. Many of us try to work day and night to keep up with our responsibilities. With so much on our plate, it is hard to let the stress go so that you can have a restful night of sleep. Instead, we stay up all night thinking about the things we need to get done!

Guided Meditation for Sleep, Relaxation, and Stress Relief can help you in numerous ways. By going through this practice, you will learn how you can get a full night's rest by relaxing your mind and body during difficult times. Sleep meditation allows you to relax your body and slow down your thoughts so you can get to sleep quicker and easier.

In this audio, I bring you through a whole journey to help you fall asleep. We start out with the association and take a relaxing trip through a forest and mountain to get you in the right mindset. Once you have slipped into meditation mode, we practice methods to help release your stress. From body image relaxation to healing relaxation, by the end, you will be drifting off to sleep as you have never been able to before.

By practicing sleep meditation, you will be able to stop the constant flow of thoughts that are created in your mind, and I will help you work through any issues you may be holding onto. Through meditation and self-hypnosis, you will soon feel perfect mentally, emotionally, and physically.

Start your sleep journey today.

Chapter 8: Countering Anxiety Through Meditation Techniques

Many people within society are facing severe issues about anxiety. Some people end up losing their lives while a good number leads to a frustrating experience for the rest of their lives. Emotionally, they are failing on how to control themselves. Usually, anxiety forms part and parcel of our emotions. Sometimes, it is healthy and falling on the positive side of your health. In this case, you may call it a good feeling. However, anxiety can build up in a person to some toxic level. You end up harboring anxiety at a disproportionate level, forcing you to make a short call at the hospital. That is a situation of a medical disorder. Your mental health starts incurring diagnoses that result in severe fear, worry, excessive nervousness, and even apprehension.

Disorders have high impacts on the behavior of someone. Your mind gets altered, and all these lead to physical symptoms, which are very severe and sometimes harsh. You start experiencing some strange emotions. Therefore, you can either have mild anxiety or severe anxiety. In the case of severe anxiety, you will emotionally suffer, and this will affect your day to day activities. However, mild anxiety has got vagueness issues plus unsettling kind of disturbances. Therefore, due to what has been so far, we can now define anxiety. Anxiety refers to an emotion embraced with wild thoughts, tension, feelings, and even physical changes such as high impulse rates. You can control and manage your anxiety in many ways, such as meeting your demands. Doing the correct thing and filling those gaps that caused you this kind of stress will help you a lot. However, you can also control the level of your anxiety through a proper step by step meditation. In this chapter, we are going to take a look at the meditation techniques you can employ or implement to counter your anxiety.

The first meditation technique in this category is **breathing.** When you are emotionally anxious, your impulse increases, leading to faster breathing. You may feel droplets of sweat at your armpits and face. You will feel lightheaded and sometimes wholly dizzy. At this moment, getting your breath at a stable level becomes a little bit difficult. There are several meditation techniques you can do to overcome the anxiety and bring your breathing under management. These include the following:

You can start by sitting in a comfortable place and completely quiet. Place your hand on the stomach and the other hand on your chest. Breathe in and out, slowly making sure your stomach moving faster than the chest.

Next, use your nose to have regular and slow breathing in and slowly breathe out using your mouth. Try as much as possible to watch your hands, sensing them more often. Your hand at the chest should not move; however, you should slightly move the other side across the stomach.

Now your anxiety is a little bit becoming weak. You can go ahead with this process as many times as you wish till you feel a little bit relaxed. At this moment, your anxiety will lessen up.

Secondly, **visualize**. In this case, you can work on your visualization state of mind. It will help you realize a happy place in your mind. Visualization paints a flowering picture in your mental mind. It comes a feeling of relaxation, and this will eventually calm and cool both of your body and brain. You are anxious, look for a comfortable place, and remain completely quiet and silent. Start having thoughts of your best site for relaxing. While you are doing this, try to think of a place that gives you peace, happiness, and more so, a calming state of mind. However, this place can be either in the real world or instead of a hypothetical situation. You should put more effort here to get the optimum level of relaxation. More so, this place should also be more comfortable to think about and use it as a future referral to all of your anxiety conditions.

Now go ahead with your visualization. Take your time to think of those small details and things you would find in that place if at all you were there. Think of the feeling of the site, how it would smell and sound. In sound, I mean all kinds of music within the happy atmosphere, and this would be caused by the following factors such as birds, movement of heavy machines, and so on. Think of the rivers flowing with a soothing sound and a cooling effect of wind breeze. Start envisioning yourself while thoroughly enjoying and making fun in that place. Now that you have this picture in your mind, you can start by closing your eyes and making some regular but slow breathes using your nose and breathing out through your mouth. Maintain both the breathing and visualization process until your anxiety starts to lessen. Since your anxious emotion will lift, do not forget to revisit this place during anxiety conditions.

You can also do exercises that relax your muscles, whether within the short run or long run. Anxiety causes tension, strain, exhaustion, and weakness of your muscles. In most cases, it is not that much; however, sometimes, this cannot allow you to concentrate on other issues. Muscle stress act as a hindrance to your anxiety management. It has that nagging and annoying trend of creating difficulty in your way to control your anxiety. Therefore, the only way to achieve your anxiety elimination is to first destroy or eradicate any element of stress within your muscles. There are several meditation exercises that you can get on your way to start the process, as you can see below. Since you want to delete muscle tension during anxiety moments, you can do the following:

☐ Look for the right comfortable place and in total silence. Make sure you have closed your eyes and concentrate on your breathing. Breathe in and out for sometimes. Make sure it is slow breathing, which you do with your nose and breathe out using your mouth.

☐Still breathing, make a tight fist using your hand and tightly squeeze your fist.
☐While still squeezing your fist, hold it for few seconds and detect all the strain and tension you are feeling now, especially in your hand.
☐Go ahead by opening your fist, note how you feel in this situation. At this juncture, you may notice some element of tension deserting you, and this reflects on your hand, resulting in a more relaxed and lighter situation.
☐You can continue doing this tensing and releasing for quite some time. Apply this in different parts of the body, such as legs, hands, feet, or even areas across your shoulders. By doing this, you will be able to delete several muscle group's tensions entirely. You can also work your way up and down and continue performing tensing and releasing. However, make sure you avoid areas with injury, if any, as this would only aggravate further your injury.

Another meditation technique you can also employ to counter anxiety is

counting. Many people always avoid it for various reasons that are funnily unknown to me even though several books of psychology talk much about it. Many psychologists, taking psychological therapy as a living or as a hobby, also are busy doing it to their clients. Counting is a simple and easy way to ease up your anxious mind. When you get yourself in that mix of anxiety, get yourself the right place; make sure it is a little bit quiet and silent. It should be comfortable too since that will create a relaxing feeling without many disturbances. After meeting up with these conditions, you can go ahead with your counting process. Start counting from one to ten, and you can go with this even up to 20 times. Counting is not limited; therefore, you can move to higher figures until you feel you are recuperating well. That is, your anxiety is lifting and subsidizing tremendously. Sometimes, you might get a quicker and faster relief; however, other times, this may prove to take a little bit longer. In this case, you should only be patient and stay calm as you focus on your emotional healing process. It is better to note that healing is a process that requires patience and time.

In most cases, the healing process is like planting a seed in the valley to sprout; then, you sit back waiting for the fruits. You will realize all these take substantial time, and only patience will help. The counting process not only reduces your anxious mind but also helps you to focus on other things. You can apply it anywhere and everywhere since it is an excellent meditation tool. You can use it while on the train or even concentrating on some duties within the store. You can also do this in any crowded place that you may get yourself. According to studies carried out recently, many psychologists recommended this since you can easily apply it anywhere and, in all areas, where other meditation exercises give you much challenge to carry out. All in all, meditation exercises can benefit everyone, and if one does not work on you, choose the next one.

Staying present is also another meditation technique that will help you counter your level of anxiety. You must look for ways to create your mindfulness at all times. That's, you should practice as hard as possible to be present in your state of mind, and no one should judge you under any circumstances. Staying in this situation will help you eradicate several groups of anxiety that might be building up. Therefore, you can at least bring back your state of mind by doing the following exercises:

☐ Look for a quiet place and make sure it is very comfortable where you can eventually sit while closing your eyes.

☐ You can as well make a note on how you feel, especially about your body, and this should be extended to your breathing too.

☐ After this, make a slight change in your awareness of your surroundings. Take every note of anything that's happening, especially in the external world. What you smell or even here will eventually bring back your physical balance in terms of your mindfulness. Again, there is that feeling of an environment that will invade your presence. This will also give you that chance of having your present state back, thus countering your anxiety.

☐ You can also change your awareness by shifting it from your environment to your body. Repeat it until your anxious mind become free, and the level of anxiety diminishes ultimately.

You can also counter anxiety by **interrupting** it. That is, interrupting your thinking here. It is always hard to have an honest thought when you have a high level of stress. Again, even less level, such as mild anxiety, instills in you that unsettling feeling that prevents you from thinking very well. Anxious thinking is hazardous since you might end up thinking of something that's not true. You end up making severe accusations followed by some critical steps in life that you might regret later on as time passes. Also, you may get yourself doing things that would only worsen your already worse situation. The only way to avoid this is by breaking the anxious thoughts that are lingering on your now stressed up mind. The following guidelines will eventually help you to come up with a clear thing far off from the anxious mind.

☐ You can start asking yourself about your usual worries and if at all these worries are complicated and offer a problem to you. If your answer is yes, then you are off to the process of starting up your meditation as quick as possible.

☐ After this, you can now start your anxiety interruptions using the following steps.

☐ You can try singing any song whether you know it or not as long as you have mastered some parts of it. Again, you can speak aloud your anxieties or try shouting or talking them to yourself.

☐ After this, think of an excellent task for your next focus instead of your anxiety. Therefore, this focus could be on your spouse, children, a person you cherish, your happy place, or even some tasks that you have saved to undertake them later on during the day, such as having a meeting somewhere.

Another way to interrupt your anxiety is by investing much of your time in listening to music or even having some excellent collections of different books touching on various life chapters.

Last but not least, on this, try as hard as possible to handle yourself with much dignity and notice your feeling after every meditation practice you undertake. Note the way your anxiety diminishes.

Another meditation technique you can also use is the **self-stress management**. Anxiety comes as a result of the stress of not getting something or not achieving something. When you learn to eliminate stress, then you will be in a position to fight off your anxiety. Again, understanding how you can manage stress help you to strike off the possible triggers of your anxious mind. You can, therefore, manage this through proper organization of your upcoming deadlines and various pressures. Do this by compiling them correctly in a manner that you can eventually achieve them. Make sure that those daunting tasks are achievable and more manageable. Still on this, you can take some time off for your benefit. Locate for yourself some free time so that you can make even a nature stroll to release some hidden anxiety.

You can also offer yourself some **relaxing techniques**. These relaxing techniques provide you that kind of meditation feeling to counter your anxiety. There are several ways in which you can have a relaxing posture in your mind, and these include breathing exercises, resting, and even staying in the dark. Yoga, long baths, and even mild slow sex are part and parcel of these relaxing techniques that are part of meditation. Breathing exercises such as breathing in through your nose and taking and taking the air out through your mouth have been seen as good ways to release the toxic level of anxiety. Long baths, especially within the bathtub, can release some tensions within your strained body. You will feel a little relaxed in the end. As a result, this will lead to the eradication of anxiety. We have slow sex and romance, too, which also contributes to the reduction of anxiety level. If well maintained and managed, the issues of anxious thoughts and worries will never be an issue. Yoga helps you not only to reduce anxiety but also a reduction in weight. Due to this, you will lead a life free from health-related complications. There are several ways to carry out your yoga activities and always struggle to get the best. If you cannot find one, then you can consult your doctor or trainer. You can also rest in the dark for longer times as expected. Darkness is a quiet, silent place with little or no disturbance at all. In this place, you can even perform other meditation techniques such as breathing, counting, and so on. You can also listen to the sounds made by several animals within the atmosphere and expose your whole body to the prevailing fresh air. All these will leave you in a situation where you are not anxious and, if any, then very minimal or little.

Other forms of meditation techniques include **performing some exercises to replace your negative thinking with**

positivity. On most occasions, anxiety comes about as a result of having some negative thoughts within your mind. You start off thinking of things that are not there, or instead of having a clear state of consciousness, you end up having a dirty mind. To start on this, you can make a good list of every bad or negative thought that lingers on your consciousness mind every day. Make a corresponding list but positive things you can eventually use to counteract the negative ones. You should make sure that these lists are manageable. There and then, establish a mental image with a notion of conquering all your fear. For example, you have worries about not completing your job today, and this has been bothering you for quite sometimes.

On the other hand, without completing your job today, you will have to forfeit the wages. The feeling of not getting paid at the end of the day gives you many worries that at the end of the day, you become highly anxious. The best positive thing to note down is how you can still have money. It seems in your worries, and money was the anxiety trigger. If you can as well get other sources of money as long as they are legit, then you will be able to avoid anxiety in this manner. This might be a short-run solution to the predicament, and next time you may think of having a long-term solution. As much as you look for an immediate solution about your worries that later on leads to anxiety, try as much as possible to get the long-term solution. A long-term solution, in this case, is to come up with a drafted plan containing a step by step guideline on how to complete that task within that located time.

There are other meditation techniques such as getting involved in **volunteering work** within your society. Society is full of life-threatening and complications that affect their day to day activities. People are suffering from a particular illness due to negligence. Others are undergoing traumas caused by fire, death of the loved ones, and much more. Some, on the other hand, need physical and emotional encouragement to keep going. So, you can eventually chip in within this society and help them solve these life disputes that seem to devour them in the next moment of their lives. Touching someone's heart has the power to accelerate their lives once more. You can also get into their contribution lists and donate a few of the items you no longer need though still in good condition. Therefore, you will realize that your anxious mind and all the worries that came with it have reduced or even eliminated.

Chapter 9: How To Start Meditating

Now that you've figured out how your body wants you to sit, and what feels natural to you for your meditation, we outline the basic steps to get you going. It is assumed that you already have a time and a place you're going to meditate that's quiet, where you won't be disturbed.

Set a timer for 10-15 minutes, depending on how long you want to meditate for. You should not meditate for longer than 15 minutes for your first few times. The timer will keep you from being distracted and worrying about the passage of time. Try and have a timer that beeps gently, as you may become more sensitive to noise.

Start your timer, and then get comfortable.

Begin by focusing on your breath. Become aware of how it moves smoothly in and out of your body. Focus on it, and the points where it switches from inhale to exhale. Imagine that your breath is moving in and out of a building, its door opening in both directions and never really closing.

You will notice thoughts pop into your head now and again, perhaps quite often at first. Your mind has a certain ebb and flow to it. Accept it, and accept yourself. Your mind and body both know what they're doing. Acknowledge the thought(s), and then bring your focus back to your breath.

If you like, you may count your breath. Start by counting every inhale and exhale as one count, separately. Try and get to ten. If your mind wanders off, start counting back at one after you've focused back on your breath. When you get to ten, start again at one.

Once you've gotten to ten in a few times, try to count each inhale and exhale together as just one count. Again, try to get to ten as described in step 5.

If you get to ten many times during step 6, try to focus purely on your breath and your body, and stop counting. Do not worry if this seems impossible. It takes time, and you will definitely get there.

That's it! The more often you meditate, the more quickly you will notice its benefits. You will notice that after a short time, you can easily get to step 7. You'll also notice that you get through the steps faster, as you learn to focus. You might then expand your practice by focusing on a word or mantra of some sort. Anything you find inspirational or motivational is a great mantra to use. Repeat the mantra silently in your head for the duration of your practice.

The hardest part of meditation is sticking with it. Many people get discouraged because they feel they "can't do it." To those feeling discouraged, let go of your expectations. Without those expectations, no-one is judging your meditation. It is only for yourself and your own benefit. If you stick to it for few months, you will get there, guaranteed.

Common Obstacles to Meditation

Creating a meditation practice goes a long way to enhancing your quality of life, spiritual growth and mental health. Let's explore common obstacles and how to overcome them.

Grasping

It is familiar to us to try to grasp at mindfulness meditation. To remember and regurgitate like we did in grade school with Math, English, etc. We grasp at the concepts to store them in our mind for later use. This is a familiar mode for us to be in. Meditation is different, it cannot be learned this way. We can read about Meditation forever, but this is not meditating. Meditation is to be experienced, it is a felt sense. So we can read about meditation as a support for our practice, but the most important element is the practice itself.

Being Hungry

Another physiological need, hunger can easily override your attempts to remain mindful. As you go from a mild urge to eat, to hunger, to feeling outright famished, you divert mental energy away from your field of awareness to the task of finding your next meal. As blood sugar continues to drop, you become susceptible to hungry's evil twin, hangry. How often have you heard (or uttered) the phrase, "I'm sorry for what I said when I was hungry"?

With your attention focused exclusively on food, there's little room for mindfulness, compassion, and enlightened thinking. It's usually only after you have eaten and your blood sugar levels return to normal do you start to feel yourself again and are able to make more conscious choices.

Having Emotional Reactivity

When you're caught up in a wave of emotion, you rarely have your mindful wits about you. Emotions can be incredibly powerful and before you know what happened, you can find yourself emotionally hijacked and totally overwhelmed by a chemical cocktail rushing through your bloodstream. The emotion experienced doesn't necessarily have to be negative; positive emotions can just as easily take you over, making mindful awareness a struggle to maintain. It's usually only after the initial tidal wave of emotion has subsided do you feel even-keeled enough to regain a little more awareness and presence.

Being Under Stress

Although it may seem obvious, it's important to recognize that when you're in the throes of either acute or chronic stress, mindfulness is quite literally the furthest thing from your mind. This is due to the fact that the fight-or-flight response is the most primitive behavior of your nervous system. By its very nature, it locks you out of the mindfulness cultivated by the restful awareness response. When the autonomic nervous system is signaling a red alert, you have exceptionally little conscious control over your state of awareness. Until you are able to down-regulate the fight-or-flight response through stress-management techniques such as breath work, meditation, or some type of physical release, accessing mindfulness will be illusive.

Being Exhausted

Consider the last time you came home from a long day at work. You're physically and mentally depleted and all you want to do is rest. This is not a mental environment conducive to being mindful.

That's because being mindful requires a certain amount of mental energy.

When your tank is empty, you just don't have the reserves necessary to keep your awareness levels up. Your mind and body allocate their energy based upon your most pressing physiological needs, and if you're wiped out, recovering your energy through sleep will take a higher priority than being mindfully aware. Higher consciousness isn't an option when all your remaining energy is being used to prevent you from becoming totally unconscious.

Experiencing Pain

The pain of any kind (physical, mental, emotional) can be overwhelming at times. In those excruciating moments, mindfulness can feel like an unreachable destination that tauntingly whispers, "You can't get there from here." The acute or chronic pain is like a roadblock that short-circuits any meaningful mental activity. Unless the pain can be managed, mindfulness requires a herculean effort to maintain during these challenging times.

This is not to say that mindfulness cannot be achieved during painful situations; indeed, mindfulness traditions encourage you to "be with" your pain, becoming deeply aware of the sensations and in doing so, you can experience it without suffering over it. Yet, pain can be one of the most challenging experiences in which to remain mindful.

Being Absorbed in Your Own Narrative

Your internal dialogue is like the narrator of your life. It weaves an ongoing ego-driven story about the roles you play, what you believe, your purpose in life, and countless other details of your day-to-day existence. While this dialogue is a normal part of life, you can often become entangled in these stories or fantasies that you sacrifice your higher self for the ego self. You may manufacture illusory debates or perform soliloquies to your internal audience completely losing sight of one key detail—none of it is real; it exists only in your mind. In these periods of self-absorbed confusion, mindfulness gets lost in the make believe construct of your ego. And the more you indulge in this fantasy, the more real it seems. However, until you reconnect with your true self, it is difficult to regain a more mindful perspective.

Having Addictive or Compulsive Behavior

Addiction is a form of attachment to pleasure that traps you in an automatic program designed to continually feed your desires. Once the preconditioned program takes over, you become increasingly mindless and chase after more of what you can't get enough of. To make matters worse, your system gets swamped in the dopamine rush of giving in to your addiction, triggering a feedback loop that becomes difficult to escape. This is why addictions and compulsive behavior can be so hard to curb—in an act of automatic self-sustaining pleasure, mindfulness is literally locked out of the system. Only through diligent practice and vigilance can mindful awareness begin to creep back in and allow for conscious choice making to override the conditioned behavior.

Trying to Shut Off the Mind

Often meditation students believe that they are unable to meditate because they are trying to shut off their mind. The goal of meditation is not to shut off your mind. One of the goals of mindfulness meditation is to recognize the belief that if we are unable to shut off our mind, we are not a "good meditator". It is the nature of the mind to wander. It is normal and expected in meditation for the mind to be busy, to lose focus or be unable to relax.

False Perception or Psychic experiences

When you practise meditation, you can expect to come to face with many subtle thoughts and visions which have been stored away in the subconscious mind. Many people feel that because they are having psychic experiences they are progressing into spirituals life. But this is not true. All psychic experiences are unreal they are not ultimate goal. They misguide our consciousness and make us forget our real path. Do not become involved with psychic experiences and do not crave for them. With careful observation they will pass away and you may never have them again.

Not Having Enough Time

The biggest obstacle people face in developing a regular meditation practice is TIME. We don't have enough time to meditate! (Interestingly enough this wasn't just an "American" phenomenon. People from all across the globe mentioned they didn't have enough time to meditate).

Yet there are simple ways to incorporate meditation into your life without taking ANY time out of your current schedule!

First, take the Don't Wait-Meditate, pledge by converting your waiting time into meditating time. The average person waits 45-60 minutes a day. We wait for appointments, we wait in traffic, we wait in line at the grocery store and we wait on hold on the phone. Yet those precious "waiting times" can be converted into meditating times.

So next time you are waiting for an appointment, take a moment to notice your breath. Or next time you are waiting in line at the grocery store, take a moment to smile from the inside. (Keep reading for simple meditation techniques you can easily incorporate while waiting).

Second, have a daily activity be your meditation. You can incorporate meditation into any of these daily activities:

Brushing your teeth
Emptying the dishwasher
Showering
Eating
Walking
Folding laundry, ironing

As you brush your teeth, notice your breath. Or notice the aliveness in your hands and mouth. As you empty the dishwasher, feel the aliveness in your hand as you put each dish away.

Third, have your dog or cat be your meditation! Have you ever noticed when walking your dog how your dog is completely in the moment, taking in its' surroundings? Well you can join your dog in this blissful state. When walking the dog notice the aliveness in your feet with each step. Notice the aliveness of the trees, birds, your surroundings. While petting the cat, notice the softness of the fur. Be completely present with your dog or cat!

Fourth, meditate while driving! Now, of course, do NOT close your eyes and meditate while driving. But you can be completely present while driving, with your eyes open. While driving, notice the aliveness in your hands as you touch the steering wheel. Or at a stop sign or in traffic, notice your breath.

These are simple ways you can incorporate meditation into your daily life without taking ANY time out of your current schedule. If we all did these simple things, we'd have a daily meditation practice!

Failure in Concentration

As the person practises concentration the suppressed or hidden mental tendencies begin to appear on the surface and drag the mind down. When the mind craves sensual stimulation it become agitated and unable to concentrate The problem lies in a weak will. You must keep your interest alive. Uninterrupted and regular practice of meditation is the remedy to this problem.

Chapter 10: 50 Daily Affirmations To Promote Positive Thinking

I am an attractive person. A positive affirmation shows up as that thing. That may from the earliest starting point sound like an immediate and void sentence to you. Notwithstanding, in the event that you repeat verifications regularly enough, your instinctual will make positive examinations. In this way, you can get the best part of the inspiration.

These days, positive affirmations are more standard than later in late memory. With Facebook, Twitter and Instagram, you can rapidly arrive at endless individuals with only a single click.

In this chapter, we will clarify what positive affirmations are, the manner by which they work in detail and how you can do day-by-day assertions to breathe life into positive musings. You will figure out how to utilize these convictions to make each life circumstance positive. Toward the finish of this chapter, you will discover a rundown of several affirmations that you can verbalize on a daily level.

What Are Positive Affirmations?

Affirmations are substantially more than simply feel great statements. They are phrases, detailed in the language of our brain.

Affirmations are certain announcements of confidence that impact our intuitive personality.

We utilize the language of the psyche to discuss straightforwardly with our mind. Affirmations must be held up and boisterous. They ought to likewise be repeated a few times to energize and fortify the individual who is expressing them.

Regardless of whether you have most likely discovered a few arrangements of solid or best affirmations on the Web, they ought to be treated with alert. The vast majority of them are not generally affirmations by any means. There are a couple of standards that these expressions must follow so as to be seen as the language of the psyche. Else, you will be baffled if these "affirmations" from the web you found do not work.

Things being what they are, our mind has severe standards with regards to speaking with the intuitive. To cause your brain to understand that you are conversing with it, you should consider the accompanying three things when characterizing amazing affirmations:

Present Tense: Positive affirmations are composed distinctly in the current state. Affirmations that start with "I will" or "I was" cannot be enrolled all things considered by your psyche.

Positive words: All together for a certification to work, it just must be made out of positive words. It is demonstrated to be progressively hard for our psyches to translate negative words in a positive manner. For what reason don't you simply state "I'm effective" rather than "I can't fall flat"?

• Facts and reality: Your psyche responds just to certainties and reality. A "possibly" or "maybe" will not be viewed as a positive insistence by your psyche. It is ideal to utilize supreme explanations dependent on actualities and truth.

To put it plainly, positive affirmations are expressions planned in the language of your mind that empowers us to speak with our subliminal through the intensity of considerations.

How Do Affirmations work?

Subsequent to clarifying what positive affirmations are, we should discuss how they work.

So as to see how they work, we first need to discuss how your mind speaks with you.

You should know ahead of time, however: Your mind can be extremely confused and complex. It transmits and gets data at the speed of light and is the principal part of our focal sensory system.

On account of the colossal measure of data that our brain needs to process each second, it takes in all that we state and think actually. The understanding happens a while later.

Daily Affirmations: Literally and in the Present Tense

Your mind does not work later at the very latest. It by and large works in the present state. We cannot feel upgrades and sentiments later on or beforehand. We can simply review or envision how we will feel.

Unbelievably, your brain is so snappy in the dynamic express that when we experience or feel something, it frames this information clearly and sends it to our body with the objective that we can set ourselves available.

For example, if you think: "Goodness, I'm going out to dinner at my favored bistro on Friday" your cerebrum interfaces with your favored restaurant definitely at this moment. So if you consider your favored bistro now, you will feel these positive sentiments in the present, and not tomorrow.

So as to make positive affirmations work, it is significant that they are constantly detailed in the present. That is the most ideal way our minds can process them. For instance, on the off chance that you state, "I land the position" before a meeting, your mind will set you up for progress at that exact instant. You will be progressively self-assured and more joyful to the outside and in this way increment your odds that you will really land the position.

Daily Affirmations: Facts and the Truth

Our cerebrum takes requests and triggers certain responses. Carefully, this is its primary capacity. Acknowledge and answer data.

Deciphering takes more time for our mind than essentially activating responses. So while it deciphers that the direction "I am not forlorn" is not negative in any way, it has just commenced the order for pity quite a while in the past.

In this manner, affirmations must be detailed totally emphatically. Else, they will not work, or in the most pessimistic scenario, they may even have the contrary impact.

For example, when you drive around in your vehicle, what do you purposely look at? The trees, the vehicles driving before you and the traffic lights. Maybe simultaneously the scene, in case it is dark to you. Nonetheless, emphatically not the bread kitchens, bistros or corner stores, isn't that so? In any case, in case you have to refuel your vehicle, all of you of an unexpected notice the administration stations. This occurs in light of the way that you intentionally deal with them.

This inside mitigates us. Through this customary isolating limit of our cerebrum, we can complete complex thinking systems. Else, we would be starting at now be totally occupied with routine assignments. The flood of information would overwhelm the mindful bit of our cerebrum and cause an over-impelling.

Precisely this is the motivation behind why affirmations must have a core interest. When they contain a "possibly" or "most likely", our mind will not arrange them as significant and sort them out. So truly attempt to concentrate on certainties and reality, so as to make positive affirmations work.

Daily Affirmations: Repetition Is the Key to Success

Another basic part of amazing affirmations is redundancy. By repeating the affirmations, we utilize the intensity of idea and inward conviction.

In the first place, it might appear to be superfluous to continue repeating the affirmations. Moreover, we have recently discovered that on the off chance that we define positive articulations in the current state, in light of certainties, that ought to be sufficient, shouldn't it?

Not exactly. Our mind works with the law of propensity. Therefore, it is dependent upon your brain to become accustomed to specific procedures and methods and to coordinate the everyday practice into your intuition.

Our psyche is intended to get us during that time productively. Each time we repeat a specific activity, we show signs of improvement. Our brain reinforces this association between the intuitive and the cognizant personality.

A genuine case of this is driving a vehicle. Initially, you may have experienced issues leaving your vehicle appropriately and needed to effectively focus on driving and traffic. Today, then again, after you have obtained enough driving knowledge, you do not effectively see the traffic any longer.

This is actually how our mind functions with positive affirmations. We enter the intuitive and disguise the announcement of the sentence until conviction.

Daily Affirmations: Say the Unpleasant

Particularly with apprentices, positive affirmations may feel like untruths. For instance, in case you are not content with your present place of employment, yet continue repeating, "I cherish my activity", it can make you feel awkward.

This happens particularly in the event that you have not increased much involvement with positive affirmations yet. Affirmations are amazing expressions for internal mending and not false proclamations or trick.

You may likewise be annoyed by the way that you are just awkward discussing this point. At the point when individuals hit a sore spot, for example, an occupation or being overweight, they rapidly will in general play down their issues. This wonder is likewise called subjective cacophony. The equivalent applies to positive affirmations.

"I adore my activity" rapidly moves toward becoming "I can gain more cash" or "I can get an advancement". Furthermore, that is totally typical. No one jumps at the chance to discuss delicate issues. Individuals love comfort.

Regardless, this is really, where positive affirmations come in. We have to wander out of our standard scope of commonality and make articulations that make us cumbersome. The nonattendance of comfort and the looking at trouble make the positive affirmations so fantastic.

Notwithstanding the way that they work with the power of conviction, yet furthermore by making you make a move as a result of an awful state. So in case, you feel ungainly deceptive yourself about a subject, you will quickly start to change things.

The affirmations must, along these lines, start definitely, where it hurts us the most. It is conceivable that you change your request or your lifestyle, decide for yourself what looks good.

The Most Effective Method to Do Day by day Affirmations

Incredible affirmations are multifunctional. You can utilize them to create positive considerations for consistently. They are all around reasonable for each aspect of our lives. Notwithstanding, a great many people use them for the accompanying subjects:

- Self-love
- Positive vitality
- Career and work
- Money and riches
- Fear and beating uneasiness
- Lose weight
- Health
- Love and association
- Self-certainty and confidence
- Success

Notwithstanding the way that you have without a doubt found heaps of courses of action of affirmations on the web, you may need to describe your own and individual systematic affirmations. This can look good if you have to test the effects of positive affirmations in solitude models, or in case you need particular affirmations for standout life conditions.

So if you have to describe your very own affirmations, there are a couple of things you should consider. Clearly, the reasons we have recently referenced above are noteworthy: Current state, positive words, and substances. In addition, there are some more choices and recommendations that we should give you on your way.

Repeat Your Affirmations

Regardless of the way that you have doubtlessly found heaps of courses of action of affirmations on the web, you may need to describe your own and individual systematic affirmations. This can look good if you have to test the effects of positive affirmations isolated models, or in case you need particular affirmations for standout life conditions.

Therefore, if you have to portray your own affirmations, there are a couple of things you should consider. Clearly, the centers we have quite recently referenced above are noteworthy: Current state, positive words, and substances. Likewise, there are some more chooses of and the proposition that we should give you on your way.

Relevant Affirmations Are the Best

There are fundamentally two kinds of positive affirmations. These are Long haul affirmations and situational affirmations. On the off chance that it ought to happen that you should require situational affirmations, there is a significant rule, which you completely need to consider.

When characterizing your insistence, consistently center around the characteristics that help you to accomplish your objective and not on the objective itself.

So on the off chance that you give the introduction of a significant deal to potential clients, you need to create whatever number of new clients as would be prudent. So which of your attributes is the most helpful for this objective? Correct, Fearlessness, Appeal, and Allure.

For this circumstance, you can describe the above with these affirmations:

"I adore myself" to help self-assurance

"I am beguiling and emanate magnetism" to upgrade your appeal and moxy

What's more, not something like:

"I'm going to make plenty of offers"

"I'm going to produce plenty of clients"

Give Your Affirmation More Expression

There is an awesome method to make your confirmation all the more dominant. Complete your talking basically by contacting the spots where you feel the cynicism. So when you state, "I adore my body", contact your stomach or other issue territories of your body.

This has two fundamental impacts. Initially, we make an alleged "muscle memory" that will interface contact with an idea. So this implies each time we contact this entry, we will think about the positive assertion without talking it out.

Furthermore, we can disguise and retain the assertion quicker in light of the fact that we utilize two detects, and not only one. Feeling fortifies hearing and quickens the way toward showing into the intuitive.

Is There Science Behind Them?

Science, yes. But no magic. Positive affirmations require customary practice on the off chance that you need to make enduring, long haul changes to the manners in which that you think and feel. Fortunately, practice and prominence of positive affirmations depends on broadly acknowledged and settled mental hypothesis.

The Psychological Theory Behind Positive Affirmations

One of the key mental hypotheses behind positive affirmations is self-affirmation theory. In this way, truly, there are exact examinations dependent on the possibility that we can keep up our feeling of self-respectability by letting ourselves know (or avowing) what we trust in positive ways.

In all respects quickly, self-trustworthiness identifies with our worldwide self-viability—our apparent capacity to control moral results and react adaptably when our self-ideal is undermined. Thus, we as people are spurred to shield ourselves from these dangers by keeping up our self-trustworthiness.

Self-Identity and Self-Affirmation

Self-affirmation hypothesis has three key thoughts supporting it. They merit having at the top of the priority list in the event that we are to see how positive affirmations work as indicated by the hypothesis.

To start with, through self-affirmation, we keep up a worldwide account about ourselves. In this account, we are adaptable, good, and equipped for adjusting to various conditions. This makes up our self-character.

Self-personality (which we are looking to keep up, as referenced previously) is not equivalent to having an unbending and carefully characterized self-idea. Rather than survey ourselves in one "fixed" way, state as an "understudy" or a "child", our self-personality can be adaptable. We can consider ourselves to be receiving a scope of various characters and jobs. This implies we can characterize achievement in various ways, as well.

For what reason is this something to be thankful for? Since it implies we can see various parts of ourselves as being sure and can adjust to various circumstances much better.

Self-affirmation hypothesis has three key thoughts supporting it. They merit having at the top of the priority list in the event that we are to see how positive affirmations work as indicated by the hypothesis.

To start with, through self-affirmation, we keep up a worldwide account about ourselves. In this account, we are adaptable, good, and equipped for adjusting to various conditions. This makes up our self-character.

Benefits of Daily Affirmations

Since we find out about the hypotheses supporting positive affirmations, here are six instances of proof from observational examinations that propose that positive self-affirmation practices can be gainful:

1. Self-affirmations have been appeared to diminish wellbeing falling apart pressure
2. Self-affirmations have been utilized successfully in mediations that drove individuals to expand their physical conduct
3. They may assist us with perceiving generally "compromising" messages with less opposition, including mediations
4. They can make us more averse to expel destructive wellbeing messages, reacting rather with the expectation to improve and to eat more products of the soil
5. They have been connected decidedly to scholastic accomplishment by moderating GPA decreases in undergraduates who get a handle of things at school.
6. Self-affirmation has been shown to lower blood pressure and rumination.

If you are enthusiastic about finding out about the displayed ideal conditions of rehearsing positive affirmations, there is an article by Critcher and Dunning that is a remarkable read. In this article, it researches the propensities by which rehearsing affirmations have been appearing to help a logically expansive estimation of self-thought.

Can They Help One's Outlook on Life?

Positive affirmations can assist us with responding in a less guarded and safe way when we are given dangers. One example that can be referred to is the fact that smokers are less pompous to realistic cigarette parcel admonitions and detailed an expectation to change their conduct.

However, for the most part, a versatile, wide feeling of self makes us stronger to troubles when they emerge. Regardless of whether it is social weights, wellbeing data that makes us feel awkward, or sentiments of rejection, a more extensive self-idea can be a very supportive thing to have.

What Is Healing Affirmation?

This sort of affirmation is a positive explanation of your physical prosperity. Advanced by creator and speaker Louise Roughage, these affirmations depend on the possibility that your considerations can impact your wellbeing to improve things. You do not need to be unwell to work on recuperating affirmations; this thought can be similar as supportive for mending enthusiastic torment in the event that you consider the thought rings with you.

Affirmations for Positive Energy

In the event that I can change my considerations, I can transform anything.

Today I will gain ground towards my objectives.

My considerations do not control me, I control my musings.

I am equipped for what I will work for.

I confide in myself, and my impulses, above any other person.

To cherish myself, is a definitive love.

To make little strides towards enormous objectives in advance.

There is no more noteworthy objective than being content with yourself.

Nobody controls how I feel about myself, however me.

To make certain is to be helpful.

No negative idea will flourish in my brain.

I am remarkable, so I will be shockingly profitable.

I trust in my indisputable potential.

I need not disturb anybody's endorsing, in any case, my own.

Keep in mind yourself. You are set up for mind-boggling things.

I am satisfying my motivation in this world.

I will accomplish mind-boggling things through little advances.

In the event that you are carefree, you are nudged.

I am grateful for what I have, paying little regard to whether it is not impeccable.

I will determinedly impact another person's day.

My brain and my heart will stay open today.

I can make my decisions, my favors.

Best Daily Affirmations for Work and Life

My most prominent battles are my most prominent exercises.

I will consistently recall that I just have power over my decisions and myself.

I will realize what I do and do not have control of. I will relinquish the last mentioned.

Continuously recall that you have enough, you do what is necessary, and above all, you are sufficient.
Be the individual that you state you need to be. It is inside your control.
I am furious. I am unafraid. I am striking.
I will love myself the manner in which that I state I need others to. They cannot accomplish for me, what I will not accomplish for myself.
Make a real existence that makes you eager to get up every day.
Continuously pick benevolence, no one can tell what somebody is experiencing.
Demonstrations of generosity do not cost a thing, however, they come back to us incredible wealth.
On the off chance that it does not serve you, cut off it from your life.
On the off chance that I wish for it, I should be eager to work for it.
I have faith in myself. I am equipped for whatever I set my psyche as well.
I can be benevolent, wild, and bold – all simultaneously.

I do not have to put anybody down, to develop myself.

I give myself consent to follow what I need.

In the event that it was simple, it would NOT be justified, despite all the trouble.

Never pass up on an opportunity to fill somebody's heart with joy. No one can really tell when you changed their day.

Always remember that you compose your very own story. So make it one you will always remember.

Exercises and insight are surrounding us in the event that we are just ready to tune in.

I as of now have all that I need.

I will express my gratefulness for those I adore every day.

I will not underestimate that individuals realize what I cherish and acknowledge them.

I discharge all the antagonism inside me and open myself up to joy and opportunity.

Which positive affirmations above did you like best?

Superseding negative contemplations with positive, sure, and stirring ones can significantly influence the tone you set for your day, and how you feel about yourself. I believe you took pleasure in these mantras and positive affirmations. My most essential wish is that they outfit you with a guide of energizing contemplations and considerations.

Chapter 11: Improve Your Relationship With Work | 10 Minutes | 1000 Words

Hello and welcome to this five-minute meditation designed to help you improve your relationship with your work. Work can be overwhelming, monotonous, or stressful sometimes, and by asking key questions about what you want from your work, you can actively change how you relate to your work life. Without being clear about your relationship with work, your past habits will dictate what happens. Our habits are not something we consciously choose most of the time, usually they are handed down to us by our family, society, and role models. To consciously choose your relationship with work you will have to be clear about what you want to experience with your work. The more you focus on what you want from your job, the more you will find that it is what you get from life.

To begin I recommend putting your nearby electronics onto do not disturb. If you are in a room, consider closing the door. This will allow you to focus on what is going on and not have any distractions pull you out of the meditation.

Consider closing your eyes. Letting the external world go. Just being present with yourself.

Relaxing into your chair or what you are resting on.

Taking the time to let go of your expectations today. Just being present with what is happening now.

Letting your breath deepen into your body. Slowing it down. Enjoying the sensation of breathing.

Bringing your awareness to how your body feels today.

Releasing any stress, tension, or worry. Letting it go. Breathing in relaxation.

I will ask you some questions now. Let your first impulses answer them. Allow this to be a fluid and fun experience if possible. Just relax into this. There are no wrong answers. You can re-listen to this meditation as many times as you need to.

If you were to look at your job with an objective perception, what about your job are you already thankful for?

Do you have any coworkers you are thankful for?

Any perks to your job that you appreciate?

Any appreciation towards the money and benefits that you receive?

Do you feel appreciation for the stability it provides?

Perhaps you just like that there is free coffee available, or that one customer you get to chat with occasionally.

Think of anything, no matter how small or how large that you are thankful for, about your job.

Bring your awareness to a day when you had a wonderful day at work. What happened on that day? If you cannot think of it, just choose a day where it was a better day at work than usual.

Pick out some ideas that pop into your head about why that day was better than other days.

Did you take some time to sleep more the night before?
Did you dress a little nicer that day?
Did you have a lovely time with friends the night before or loved ones?
Did you joke around a lot with coworkers or friends online?
Did you just feel like you were in a good mood?
Pick out some elements about your day that you feel contributed positively to that good work day.
Are any of these things repeatable on your own? Could you take any of these things and repeat them perhaps once a week, just for yourself?
Is there anything about your work that you are proud of?
Are you proud of the service that you provide to others or to your company?
Are you proud of how hard you work?
Are you proud of the work you have created and provided others, no matter how small?
Are you proud that you held the door open for that one person that one day?

No matter what it is, what about your work are you proud of?
What has this job taught you about life?
Are you thankful for that lesson?
What has this job taught you about yourself?
Are you thankful for that lesson?
What is something positive that you have learned from this job?
Are you thankful for that lesson?
What is something that you will always respect about this job?
Are you thankful for that lesson?
What about this job might you carry with you for the rest of your life that is positive?
Is there anything about your relationship with this job that you would like to improve upon? Would you perhaps like to come in earlier? Would you perhaps like to eat healthier food at work? Would you perhaps like to learn healthy work-life balance? Take some time to ponder about what could work even more in your favor.
Keeping your breathing at a gentle pace.

Are there any tiny changes you can do on a daily basis that would allow your work to be more positive and happy for you?

Are there any tiny changes you could make that could allow you to experience a better work day?

Would you be willing to do those tiny changes every day to make your work life better?

Keeping your breathing going at a slow and gentle pace.

And as the last thing to explore, if you could have a wonderful day at work every day, what would you need to change about yourself in order to do that? Is there any habit or perception that may need to be altered as you move forward? Be gentle with yourself. Go with little steps you could change. Perhaps waking up five minutes earlier. Perhaps eating one more vegetable serving per day. Go very small.

Sometimes in order to change your external reality, you must change your internal reality first. By changing your relationship to work, you can change how your work interacts with you. As the day goes by, keep thinking of things you are grateful for about your work. The more you look at what is going right, the more things will start to work out in your favor.

Thank you for listening to this meditation today. Have a wonderful work day.

Simple Relaxation for a Busy Day | 10 Minutes | 991 Words

Hello and welcome to this meditation for a simple relaxation for a busy day. Just take a moment to relax and let these words flow over your mind. Have fun with it.

Breathing in and out at a pace that feels comfortable for your body.

Letting anything go that arises within you.

Breathing in, and letting the cool air enter into your body.

Breathing everything out, and letting all the heavy, stagnant, and unreleased air out on the exhalations.

Allow your mind to let go of its thoughts.

Allow your body to let go of its pain or tension.

Allow your emotions to soften.

Breathing deeply as you do this.

Allowing all of your tense energy to leave your body into the Earth beneath you.

Allowing all of your tension to leave through the very bottom of your feet.

Allowing all of your tension to leave through the bones in your feet.

Allowing all of your tension to leave through the muscles of your feet.

Allowing all of your tension to leave through the skin of your feet.

Allowing all of your tension to leave through the bones of your ankles.

Allowing all of your tension to leave through the muscles of your ankles.

Allowing all of your tension to leave through the skin of your ankles.

Allowing all of your tension to leave through the bones of your lower legs.

Allowing all of your tension to leave through the muscles of your lower legs.

Allowing all of your tension to leave through the skin of your lower legs.

Allowing all of your tension to leave through the bones of your knees.

Allowing all of your tension to leave through the muscles of your knees.

Allowing all of your tension to leave through the skin of your knees.

Allowing all of your tension to leave through the bones of your upper legs.

Allowing all of your tension to leave through the muscles of your upper legs.

Allowing all of your tension to leave through the skin of your upper legs.

Allowing all of your tension to leave through the bones of your pelvic and hip area.

Allowing all of your tension to leave through the muscles of your pelvic and hip area.

Allowing all of your tension to leave through the skin of your pelvic and hip area.

Allowing all of your tension to leave through the bones of your stomach and waist area.

Allowing all of your tension to leave through the muscles of your stomach and waist area.

Allowing all of your tension to leave through the skin of your stomach and waist area.

Allowing all of your tension to leave through the bones of your rib cage.

Allowing all of your tension to leave through the muscles of your rib cage.

Allowing all of your tension to leave through the skin of your rib cage.

Allowing all of your tension to leave through the bones of your chest and upper back.

Allowing all of your tension to leave through the muscles of your chest and upper back.

Allowing all of your tension to leave through the skin of your chest and upper back.

Allowing all of your tension to leave through the bones of your shoulders.

Allowing all of your tension to leave through the muscles of your shoulders.

Allowing all of your tension to leave through the skin of your shoulders.

Allowing all of your tension to leave through the bones of your upper arms.

Allowing all of your tension to leave through the muscles of your upper arms.

Allowing all of your tension to leave through the skin of your upper arms.
Allowing all of your tension to leave through the bones of your elbows.
Allowing all of your tension to leave through the muscles of your elbows.
Allowing all of your tension to leave through the skin of your elbows.
Allowing all of your tension to leave through the bones of your lower arms.
Allowing all of your tension to leave through the muscles of your lower arms.
Allowing all of your tension to leave through the skin of your lower arms.
Allowing all of your tension to leave through the bones of your hands.
Allowing all of your tension to leave through the muscles of your hands.
Allowing all of your tension to leave through the skin of your hands.
Allowing all of your tension to leave through the bones of your neck.
Allowing all of your tension to leave through the muscles of your neck.
Allowing all of your tension to leave through the skin of your neck.

Allowing all of your tension to leave through the bones of your face.
Allowing all of your tension to leave through the muscles of your face.
Allowing all of your tension to leave through the skin of your face.
Allowing all of your tension to leave through the bones of your head.
Allowing all of your tension to leave through the muscles of your head.
Allowing all of your tension to leave through the skin of your head.
Allowing all of your tension to leave through the bones of your whole body.
Allowing all of your tension to leave through the muscles of your whole body.
Allowing all of your tension to leave through the skin of your whole body.
Just taking some time to be present with where your body is now, compared to where it was before.
Breathing in... and out...
Coming back into the sensation of hearing the sounds around you.
Coming back into the sensation of smelling the scents around you.

Coming back into the sensation of tasting any flavors on your tongue.

Coming back into the sensations of your body.

Coming back into the sensation of seeing any colors, shapes, or light vs. shadow around you.

Coming back into where you are right now. Your environment. Your surroundings.

Thank you for listening to this meditation today. Have a peaceful day.

Conclusion

By now, you've had a clear comprehension that insomnia is a brutal sleeping disorder that afflicts millions of people around the globe each year. It knows no bounds of age, gender, race, ethnicity, or status; it has become a widespread problem. Insomnia's repercussions transcend the realms of night time and end up affecting the daytime severely as well. Over the years, scientists and researchers have struggled and set out to find plausible causes for this sleeplessness epidemic. Even though there is no one clear cause identified, there has been a discovery that many causes work in tandem to manifest insomnia and other sleeping disorders.

Furthermore, insomnia is basically a sleep disorder, which means it has many other scary cousins, namely sleepwalking, narcolepsy, sleep apnea, Restless Leg Syndrome (RLS). Most of the time, the same risk factors and causes that lead to these disorders also lead to insomnia.

Hence, it is imperative to understand the causal factors behind sleeping disorders.

According to research, the biggest culprits behind insomnia are stress, depression, and anxiety. In this ever-growing, fast-paced 21st century world, it's only natural to have anxiety and tension in your life. Most of the people cannot unwind and relax their racing minds when they go to bed every night. They are unable to let go of the regrets in the past and worries of the future. Therefore, they find it hard to fall asleep, or if they do, cannot stay asleep¾a hallmark symptom of insomnia. In addition, old age, being female, certain medications like OTC drugs for histamine allergies, ADHD drugs, hypertension, and diabetes, etc. also cause insomnia. Furthermore, certain medical conditions like gastric reflux, allergic rhinitis, overactive thyroid, chronic pain, neurological disorders like Parkinson's disease also make it difficult to have a good night's sleep. Moreover, having poor sleep hygiene is a surefire way to ward off sleep. It includes bad lifestyle choices like doing heavy physical activity right before going to bed, using smart screens around bedtime or in bed, consuming too much caffeine throughout the day, or lying awake in bed during daytime

Fortunately, there are many remedies to help with insomnia. The best remedy so far to calm the "monkey mind" at night is meditation. You can practice guided or unguided meditation, depending on whichever suits you best. However guided meditations are much easier to do on your own and cost absolutely nothing. Therefore, they are always preferred and recommended by sleep specialists all over the world. Guided meditation does wonders for insomniacs, but it does it is even more wonderful.

.

www.ingramcontent.com/pod-product-compliance
Lightning Source LLC
Chambersburg PA
CBHW050506120526
44589CB00046B/948